"The book skillfully embeds complex ideas about civic leadership in five well-told stories of individuals who chose to work toward goals well beyond the scope of their formal positions. In so doing, it illustrates the personal and human work of civic leadership in ways that inspire others to engage and gives a clear-eyed appraisal of the required effort and accompanying risks."

G. Thomas Bellamy, Professor of Education and Director, Goodlad Institute for Educational Renewal, University of Washington Bothell

"Anyone who cares about encouraging healthy communities will profit from the theoretical analysis and inspiring case studies in For the Common Good. *Chrislip and O'Malley celebrate the courage and effective adaptive strategies creative leaders learn in the trenches of community service."*

Thomas E. Cronin, Colorado College and co-author of *Leadership Matters*

"The Kansas Leadership Center works ambitiously to shape the statewide leadership of civil society. For the Common Good *explains what KLC is trying to do and its thoughtful approach that centers on intra- and inter-personal competencies necessary to implement the KLC's five principles of leadership. Their effort and this work deserve the attention of everyone interested in democratic governance!"*

Richard Couto, Distinguished Senior Scholar, Union Institute & University

"With its elegant writing, insightful analysis of the political context and comprehensive leadership framework for making progress, this book is a major contribution to the concept of civic leadership and beyond."

John Goodlad, author of *A Place Called School*

"Chrislip and O'Malley have uniquely combined intellect, storytelling, and provocative questions that inform and challenge readers interested in the practice of civic leadership. Intrigued by the concept of adaptive work, I intend to use this book in my graduate class on facilitative leadership and citizen engagement."

John Nalbandian, University of Kansas School of Public Affairs and Administration

"Chrislip and O'Malley call for a radical shift in how we think about civic leadership and in the skills that we should encourage in leaders. Drawing on their deep knowledge of the field and their own first-hand experience training a new generation of civic leaders, their book provides a compelling argument for adaptive leadership, enriched with true-to-life case studies that illustrate the grueling, yet essential nature of this work."

Doug Easterling, Associate Professor and Department Chair, Wake Forest University School of Medicine

"For the Common Good *is a must-read for leadership scholars and educators to learn from the most innovative, potent and ambitious initiative ever developed to enhance community leadership. This book is even more important for those with the desire to be more impactful leaders as they will learn through the inspired and gritty stories of those who are making their communities better through their participation in the Kansas Leadership Center."*

Greg Meissen, Professor of Psychology,
Wichita State University

"For the Common Good *tells the story of civic leadership by delicately walking the line between theory and practices. The book belongs in higher education classrooms focused on civic issues and in community groups working to make progress on daunting problems."*

Tim Steffensmeier, Department Head,
Kansas State University Department
of Communication Studies

"Purposeful, intentional, empowering and accessible. This book provides us as ordinary citizens with powerful examples and tools that can help us make progress on complex issues that we care about."

Jill Arensdorf, Chair and Assistant Professor,
Fort Hays State University Department
of Leadership Studies

"Drawing both on previous leadership literature and powerful examples from politics, religion, health care and the world of nonprofits, Chrislip and O'Malley offer a transformative conception of leadership in their book, For the Common Good: Redefining Civic Leadership. *The authors aspire that their text will inspire all citizens to understand that leadership is an activity, not a position and that anyone can lead, anytime. I highly recommend this readable and provocative text."*

David E. Procter, Director, Kansas State University Center for Engagement and Community Development

"This book is a window into the practice of civic engagement. It tells stories of people like us trying to bring about change. It is also a case for why and how leadership is the work of all of us."

Stephen Fawcett, Kansas Health Foundation Professor of Community Leadership and Director, University of Kansas Work Group for Community Health and Development

FOR THE COMMON GOOD

Redefining Civic Leadership

DAVID D. CHRISLIP
and
ED O'MALLEY

KLC PRESS

KLC Press
Kansas Leadership Center
300 N. Main, Suite 100, Wichita, Kansas 67202

Visit our website at *www.kansasleadershipcenter.org*

This edition published in 2013.

Library of Congress Cataloging-in-Publication Data

Chrislip, David D., 1943-
For the common good: redefining civic leadership/
David D. Chrislip & Ed O'Malley; foreword by Marty Linsky.
p. cm.
Includes index.
ISBN: 978-0-9889777-0-9 (pbk.)
ISBN: 978-0-9889777-1-6 (e-book)
1. Community leadership—United States. 2. Civic improvement.
3. Leadership—Philosophy. 4. Community development—United States—Citizen participation. I. O'Malley, Ed. II. Linsky, Martin. III. Title.
HM1261 .C47 2013
303.3`4—dc23

Cover designed by Clare McClaren, Novella Brandhouse
Cover painting by Don Gore
Book design by Patrick Hackenberg

Printed in the United States of America

This book is dedicated to two people who worked across boundaries for the common good:

Sister Kathleen O'Malley, 1930–2011

John Parr, 1948–2007

Table of Contents

Foreword

Marty Linsky

The Kansas Leadership Center is unlike any leadership initiative I have ever seen. The mission is to create healthy communities in Kansas more capable of and willing to address their most intractable issues by nurturing the quantity and quality of civic leadership. The idea is so compelling that in November 2012, over 60 people from around the world came to Wichita, Kansas, as individuals and teams to engage with each other for a weekend of conversation about large-scale civic leadership development. Using the KLC experience as a backdrop and template, participants from such disparate locales as Nigeria, Ireland, Canada, Singapore, Japan, Mexico, Norway, France, India, The Netherlands, Australia, and over a dozen different states in the U.S. worked on strategies for similar efforts in their home settings. They must be onto something at KLC.

Thinking about what KLC is trying to do in Kansas brings to mind the incisive but discouraging column David Brooks wrote in *The New York Times* (October 16, 2012)[1] shortly before the 2012 presidential election. Brooks described the 10 qualities needed for leadership and in doing so frames the challenges David Chrislip and Ed O'Malley are grappling with in this book. He's looking at what it will take to break through the highly partisan roadblocks that prevent finding common ground in Washington. Brooks makes irrefutable what the authors already know: that civic leadership is risky, difficult

[1] Brooks, David. "Rules for Craftsmen." *New York Times.* October 16, 2012. New York Edition, p. A31.

and unlikely to come from the political class, especially anytime close to an election.

In this book, Chrislip and O'Malley are on a different journey. For them, civic leadership is available to anyone, independent of role or position. If you look at Brooks' 10 qualities, he seems to agree. There's nothing there about having a big job.

Moreover, the insight that animates this book is that the responsibility for enabling the politicians to do the right thing lies not with them, but with each of us and our commitment to and skill at civic leadership. (And, concomitantly, the politicians' failure to exercise leadership is our failure to demand it from them, reward them for it and create the conditions where they can do so.)

O'Malley is the founding president and CEO of the Kansas Leadership Center. Chrislip has been with KLC since its inception in 2007 as a critical thought partner, trusted adviser and nurturer of faculty talent among other roles.

You might be familiar with them if KLC has touched you or, since they both had distinguished careers pre-KLC, from one of their previous incarnations in public life. Then you will be delighted to read this book and see the documentation and contextualization of what you already know something about.

If you don't know them and don't know the KLC story, yet care about whether your neighborhood, community, region or country can deal with the complex, rapidly changing set of public challenges facing all of us wherever we live, then this book will give you stories, principles, frameworks, tools and, most important, a much-needed dose of hope, leavened with a hard-headed sense of what it will take to help you make progress on whatever concerns or issues you care most deeply about.

Nevertheless, as O'Malley and Chrislip point out, using large-scale leadership development as a pathway to increased and increasingly skillful civic leadership, which itself is relevant only as a means to the end of deep public transformation, is no easy task. Doing leadership development on a large scale with such ambitious goals is, in the language the authors use, an adaptive challenge. That means designing the initiative so KLC embodies the values and processes it is nurturing in others and struggles with all the assumptions and barriers that parallel the powerful forces within ourselves and within communities that are committed to the status quo.

In an important sense, the story you will read in the following pages is an example of the post-ideological, post-partisan perspective to which many people give aspirational lip service but not much else. The story of KLC, the five guiding principles it espouses and the four civic leadership competencies it has identified and shared, encompasses a commitment to a conservative notion of evolutionary, not revolutionary, change and a more liberal idea of the democratization of civic life.

All of that brings us back to David Brooks' column and the leadership challenges presented by a democratic society. I believe in politics and democracy as, in the oft-quoted words of Winston Churchill, "the worst form of government except for all those others that have been tried."

As Walter Lippmann made clear in his seminal book *Public Opinion*, written 90 years ago, democracy and politics can only function well with an engaged and aware civic community. Lippmann believed that was unachievable. Fortunately for all of us, O'Malley and Chrislip have not abandoned that noble ideal.

In this book and in the KLC experience, they have given it new life by combining a relentless belief that change is possible with a ruthless realism about what it will take to make progress on the most difficult public challenges ahead. If you care enough to want to change the world or any little piece of it, you have much to learn in the pages that follow.

New York City
January 7, 2013

Introduction

We've written this book because we believe civic leadership has far more potential to respond to today's civic challenges than its current practice allows. It's clear to us that civic leadership can become more purposeful, provocative and engaging and, thus, enhance our collective capacity to address the complex adaptive challenges we face.

Other scholars and critics have written cogently about the limitations of leadership in the public and civic realms. Some have extended their critique to include a vision of how things should be, describing in great detail the longed-for progress that always seems just out of reach. Few, however, described or defined in depth the fundamental nature of the leadership it will take to realize these elusive aspirations.

Our title, *For the Common Good,* suggests its orientation. Rather than viewing the exercise of leadership in the civic arena as a way of furthering individual desires or acting only when our backyards are threatened, we see it as a means of sharing responsibility for acting together in pursuit of the common good. In the end, limiting one's conception of the meaning of civic responsibility to a reactive or passive role most often allows for a lot of noisy complaining while leaving the responsibility for taking initiative and action to others or to local authorities. A great deal more than complaining is needed from many more of us if we're to make progress on the issues we care about.

In these pages, you will find our assessment of the current state of civic leadership along with a framework for the more powerful kind of leadership we believe necessary to respond to these conditions. Our purpose is both to redefine civic leadership and to understand how its practice can help transform the civic culture of our communities and regions. To this end, we have organized the book in three parts.

In *Part I: The State of Civic Leadership,* we begin with the story of the Kansas Leadership Center and how it originated and developed as a laboratory for learning about civic leadership. We then share the ideas of leadership thinkers that influenced our work followed by our analysis of the nature of civic challenges and their implications for leadership.

Part II: The Practice of Civic Leadership introduces four competencies of civic leadership that respond to today's civic challenges. In each chapter, we use stories from civic activists to illustrate the competencies followed by some contemplative questions to help you take what we hope will be the next steps in your own leadership journey. Here you will see stories of exemplars that reflect the kind of participants we recruit into KLC programs: individuals with some authority or influence within or between sectors or factions. Our purpose is to help them learn how to exercise leadership beyond the boundaries of their authority in the civic realm. We recognize that stories of individuals exercising leadership with little or no authority would also be illustrative. We will come back to these stories in a future work.

In the last section, *Part III: The Heart of Civic Leadership,* we suggest what it will take from you to learn how to become more effective at exercising civic leadership, and in the final chapter we return our focus to the book's title — *For the Common Good* — to explore how to realize the full potential of civic leadership.

The leadership framework we offer brings together two powerful ideas about civic work and leadership, one conservative and one liberal. First, the concept of adaptive work is a historically conservative idea, one that implies that change is evolutionary rather than revolutionary, incremental rather than radical. Adaptive work also requires the pragmatic approach of experimentation and learning one's way into progress rather than making wholesale changes on a grand scale. These ideas go back at least to the 16th century and the Italian political thinker Machiavelli followed by Irish statesman Edmund Burke two centuries later. More recently, commentators William Buckley, George Will and David Brooks have revisited these conservative themes.

The second, perhaps more liberal, idea informing our work is the critical need to democratize leadership. To make progress, many more people from diverse walks of life can, should and must exercise leadership in the civic arena in more effective ways than they have in the past. Just as the great social movements of the 1960s and 1970s opened new possibilities for civic engagement, now is the time to open new possibilities for civic leadership. Leadership cannot remain the exclusive domain of those in positions of authority or influence.

Our understanding that adaptive work requires engaging others to make progress weaves together those two philosophical threads. To be effective, civic leadership must focus on mobilizing and energizing others to take up this difficult work. These aspects reflect more democratic and inclusive notions of what this leadership must entail and who must exercise it in order to respond to the adaptive nature of the challenges.

Out of its belief that civic leadership, broadly defined, could help foster healthier, more prosperous communities across the state, in 2007 the Kansas Health Foundation created the Kansas Leadership Center. This book grew out of our learning and experiences in that new leadership development endeavor. Through those experiences, and like civic leadership itself, we know the ideas put forth in this book are not for the dispassionate. We've written it for anyone who cares enough about his community or her region to want to make a difference. Using real-life stories of civic leadership in action, we describe and illustrate the principles and competencies of that more purposeful, provocative and engaging kind of leadership.

We're certain these subtle, powerful, risky and challenging-to-put-into-practice ideas and concepts can help you become more conscious and intentional about the way you exercise civic leadership, and thus help you make more progress on the concerns you care about.

Join us on this journey for the common good.

Part I

The State of Civic Leadership

Chapter 1
A Laboratory for Civic Leadership

On a cool, blustery day in the late fall of 2007, a small group met in a room at the back of the former Occidental Hotel in Wichita, Kansas. Once hailed as the best hotel west of the Mississippi, the 19th-century building now housed the offices of the young Kansas Leadership Center (KLC). The symbolism in the connection of the state's historic civic vitality with the rejuvenating energy of KLC's purpose was not lost on our little group of five. Following 11 months of meetings, discussions and traveling the state for countless hours of intensive listening to its citizens, we'd gathered to assess the wealth of data collected and address the question of how best to implement the Center's purpose. That purpose, never far from the front of our minds, was to develop leadership to serve the common good and foster healthier communities by addressing the state's most formidable challenges; without question, we understood this was no small task.

Those of us seated around the table that day shared the belief that the root of civic leadership in the 21st century lay in mobilizing people to make progress on vital issues, a task that could be accomplished only through following a critical, though not easy, set of purposeful actions. That belief constituted the foundation of our commitment to define and develop those behaviors just as it continues to inform the Center's mission today. Indeed, the work begun in Kansas continues, but its application for exercising effective leadership for the common good now reaches far beyond the state's borders.

Putting these ideas about civic leadership into practice in Kansas as well as in other settings provides the impetus for this book.

Before delving into a more formal discussion of what has shaped KLC's philosophy and the concepts underlying its work, we think knowing something of the Center's lineage will enhance an understanding of what readers will find in these pages. What follows, then, is the first in a series of stories this book tells.

This story begins back in the 19th century when Kansans were on the cutting edge of ambition and civic leadership. Unlike Iowa, the Dakotas, Illinois, Indiana, Colorado and other states that were founded based on geography during the decades before and after Kansas statehood in 1861, the state was founded for a cause: freedom. When Congress passed the Kansas and Nebraska Act in 1854, the choice between being a free state or a slave state was left to the residents of those territories. Abolitionists from Massachusetts and elsewhere mobilized tremendous resources and numbers of people to flood the Kansas Territory with the intent that it would enter the Union as a free state. Their success helped put Kansas on the right side of history. American historian Carl Becker aptly put it this way in 1910: "The origin of Kansas must ever be associated with the struggle against slavery. Of this fact Kansans are well aware .... It is a state with a past,"[1] and "the devotion to the state [was] a devotion to an ideal, not a territory."[2]

Becker goes on to capture the provocative spirit of the state's civic leadership at the time: "Insurgency is native in Kansas and the political history of the state, like its climate, is replete with surprises that have made it alternately the reproach and the marvel of mankind."[3] From John Brown's rebellion just before the Civil War to the American Progressive movement in the late 19th century and early 20th century, this insurgent spirit caught the attention of residents and outsiders alike. Pulitzer Prize–winning newspaper editor William Allen White, the "Sage of Emporia," stood up for small-town ideals and fought corruption in governments, large or small. For most of the first 100 years after statehood, Kansans, justifiably proud of their record of civic activism, continued to be full of optimism about their state and its possibilities. Looking back, many of those efforts, while original and ahead of the time, may appear today as moralistic, overzealous, or even ornery, but they were innovative and cannot be faulted for lack of aspiration. Kansans liked to set about to improve their world, and they thought they knew how to do it. They didn't hesitate to declare something wrong, aggressively assert what should be done and, if necessary, impose their views on backsliders and ne'er-do-wells.

Given such a deep, robust civic history, one would think Kansas would be well positioned to make progress on the important issues of the present moment. The reality is that, today, the Sunflower State, like any other state, faces myriad challenges: severe economic changes accelerated by the pressures of globalization, rural population shifts to urban and suburban areas, immigration, concerns about the increasing costs of health care and concerns over educational outcomes and school reform. It's not that Kansans haven't risen to address these issues through the years — they have and still do — but like citizens elsewhere, they tend to wait until there is a crisis to act.

Unfortunately, unlike in the aftermath of a destructive tornado, flood or fire, the massive outpouring of compassionate, civic-minded action that often follows such a crisis otherwise rarely occurs. Americans know how to rebuild after these sorts of disasters but often seem clueless about how to address more complex, daunting, and persistent day-to-day civic challenges. With all good intentions, governors appoint commissions and task forces that wind up rehashing the same ideas. Or disgruntled executives offer solutions developed for business success, only to find those solutions woefully inadequate in the civic sector. Ordinary citizens in Kansas and other states across America, more or less oblivious to the challenges facing their state, defer to those in authority to solve them. Such deference and apathy — a creeping crisis of diminishing civic participation — offer no help in making progress on the unyielding, hard to grasp, and still harder to address civic challenges facing a community or region. Instead, these dispiriting qualities contribute to a slow and steady — some would say chronic — state of civic decline. Optimism seems less plentiful these days. All states need more from their residents: more commitment, higher aspirations and many more people acting together to serve the broader good. We believe Kansans, along with citizens in other states, would do well to take a page from how those hardy Kansas forebears approached things.

Some years later in the state's story came a game-changing organization, the Kansas Health Foundation. Back in 1912 citizens in Wichita built a hospital. Organized, supported and developed by Methodists, Wesley Hospital's creation represented a significant undertaking. Wichita was a booming young town but still lacked many community services; the hospital, by filling one of those gaps, aimed to improve the health of Kansans. Over time it became a major medical center serving much of Kansas and Oklahoma.

In 1985, the Board of Trustees of the nonprofit hospital, now Wesley Medical Center, sold the institution to the Hospital Corporation of America. By law, the proceeds from such sales are required to go to a nonprofit purpose. This led to the creation of the Kansas Health Foundation. After years of experience investing in improving the health of Kansans, the foundation concluded that civic leadership — broadly defined — was also critical to making progress. To put this thinking into action, KHF invested an initial $30 million over 10 years to found the Kansas Leadership Center.

The people at KLC tend to think of that $30 million as an indirect investment from those good, caring citizens of Wichita who surely struggled to build their hospital back in 1912. A century later, that investment is shepherded by a similar group of good, caring Kansans who set the direction of the Kansas Health Foundation.

These citizens left a powerful legacy and, a century after their inspiring act of civic leadership, the fruit of their hard work continues to help build stronger, healthier, more prosperous communities. We at KLC believe that we are honoring those earlier Kansans and echoing their worthy efforts through our professional mission.

At KLC, many of our programs begin with the question "How should we begin?" This usually surprises participants because they assume that the faculty should — *will* — provide the answer. More surprising to them is the expectation, emerging from the long silence that often follows the question, that they themselves must answer it.

As members of the KLC management team in its earliest days, we asked ourselves that same question. A similar long silence followed as we contemplated where and how, exactly, to get started. At that point, we felt we needed some sort of compass to help us chart the course of the work that needed to be done. Our thinking was that a deeper, hands-on analysis of the state's civic context could point us in the right direction. Accordingly, we set out on a months-long listening tour, crisscrossing the state to talk formally and informally with as many people as possible. From subject-matter experts to everyday community members, we engaged citizens in discussions about civic leadership in Kansas. Our first question was always, "When you think about the future of Kansas, what concerns you the most?" and was followed by "What are the driving forces affecting your concern?" After those two questions came more broad-based inquiries: "What in the civic culture of Kansas helps address your concerns? What hinders?" And talk to us the people did.

Among our questions were more specific ones about the creation of the Center that helped us think through what KLC should do. We wanted ideas about logistical issues such as where KLC should be located and whom it should serve, as well as more philosophical ideas about what and how the organization should teach Kansans about civic leadership. All of these questions were open and on the table at that point. The seemingly limitless number of options coupled with no easy or immediately obvious approaches made our job quite formidable. Listening well is no easy task, but adhering to Will Rogers' admonition to "never miss a good chance to shut up" kept our team focused and helped us avoid the natural tendency to start planning, strategizing or persuading others about ideas we had ourselves.

From the interviews and focus groups asking citizens to identify civic concerns and the barriers and challenges they faced when attempting to address them came clarity about the civic norms and practices of Kansans. In significant ways, the findings from that state-specific process mirrored patterns found in similar assessments across the United States. A number of troubling motifs about civic concerns and civic culture stood out. We listened as Kansans spoke with weary cynicism of inadequate progress on issues like health and health care, education, economic development, immigration, crime and the environment. Ever insightful, they understood that these issues were complex, interconnected and often polarizing, and that they affected nearly everyone. They fretted about symptomatic and reactive responses to those persistent challenges, acknowledging that superficial, stopgap solutions quickly lose effect and leave festering problems and mounting frustration. Taken as a composite, Kansans portrayed a singularly unimaginative and unproductive civic culture in which deference to authority and government, the shirking of civic responsibility, widespread complacency and apathy have eroded historic norms of trust, tolerance and reciprocity in the general population. It also became apparent that Kansans stumble woefully when attempting to address common concerns; civic leadership practices that thwart engaging, mobilizing and energizing others simply cannot inspire collective action on challenges that require mutual learning and adaptation. A stark picture, indeed.

We knew that to realize the Kansas Health Foundation's charge, the young KLC would have to respond to this analysis with ideas and programs that directly addressed those troubling patterns. By the end of our canvassing in 2007, it seemed plain enough to us that civic leadership as it was currently practiced in the state, and in America as a whole, would not be enough to help Kansans move ahead on the issues the many people we spoke to cared about. Unless many more citizens could be inspired to exercise leadership in more purposeful, provocative and engaging ways in the service of the common good, progress would remain elusive and illusory. We knew we needed to respond to the voices of Kansans in a deeply meaningful way and that our response would involve mobilizing countless people from all walks of life to act. A central task of our organization would be to define and develop the hard-to-come-by skills necessary to accomplish that. The nitty-gritty specifics of how to do this work remained an open question.

Our purpose in that late-fall 2007 meeting in the old Occidental Hotel was to convert the wealth of data generated from our listening tour into a theory of civic leadership that would focus and shape the strategies of the new organization. Among the five people seated at the table that day were the two of us, Ed, a former Republican state legislator and the first president of KLC, and David, who for 30 years through his associations with the National Civic League, the Institute for Civic Leadership and the American Leadership Forum had wrestled with the question of how best to develop civic leadership. Also present were prominent leadership consultant and teacher Marty Linsky, an edgy New Yorker used to pushing people to higher levels of self-awareness and motivation to lead, who prodded us relentlessly to deepen our aspirations; Matt Jordan, trained in city management and experienced in local politics, who kept the meeting focused and organized while offering insights from his own years of civic work; and Patty Clark, a veteran of public administration in state government with a deep understanding of partisan politics, who, when the group's imagination strayed too far afield, kept the conversation grounded in the realities of the Kansas civic context.

To that group, the imperatives for what KLC would have to do to respond to Kansas' predicament were clear enough. We began by taking the long view toward our organization's and the state's future. Some years hence, we agreed, the fruits of the Kansas Health Foundation's investment ought to be apparent in at least three dimensions. To fulfill the Foundation's vision, KLC's efforts to develop civic leadership should lead to demonstrable progress on the identified civic challenges of health, education, economic development, environment and governance. The amount of a particular kind of social capital, *bridging social capital,* the capacity of people to work together across boundaries, we believed, should grow significantly in the state. In addition, we felt the combination of more bridging social capital with more purposeful, provocative and engaging civic leadership should transform the civic culture of Kansas and its communities, bringing people together in ways that heal rather than divide.

We were well aware that this was bold and compelling work. No one in the group aspired to anything less for ourselves or for Kansans. We didn't want people simply to talk about leadership; we wanted them to learn and practice new behaviors in that realm, and we intended for *them* to transform their communities. Each of us recognized that to realize these goals, the organization's strategies would have to be aggressive and multidimensional. Despite the magnitude of the

Foundation's generous bequest, those resources would have to be leveraged by mobilizing other leadership development organizations to share the work. To extend its work across the state, KLC would have to provide powerful leadership development experiences that would meet different needs. We envisioned that some programs would be designed to address the leadership challenges inherent in specific roles as varied as school superintendents, city managers, legislators and nonprofit and business executives. Other programs would be open to anyone, offering any Kansan an opportunity to enhance his or her civic leadership capacities. Because we understood that KLC could never reach into every region and community on its own, we also intended our programs to act as support and inspiration for existing place-based community programs. The synergistic power of working at each of these levels might, just might, we believed, have a chance at truly transforming the civic culture of the state.

At the individual level, we knew that our programs would have to be eminently compelling to participants. To transform the state's civic culture, the Center's program experiences would themselves have to be transforming, calling forth the best in participants and moving them to higher levels of commitment and efficacy. We agreed that the KLC faculty would have to embody the same leadership behaviors they hoped to inspire in others. Fittingly, KLC's first program in July 2008 was designed to develop a core group of powerful teachers — Kansans inspiring Kansans — to lead its programs. Our belief was, and remains, that coupling powerful teachers with powerful ideas leads to powerful programs. This has proven to be the case through the early years of KLC's work. Certainly, no ordinary leadership development experience could inspire 1,000 people or more every year to take up the mantle of civic leadership.

The story of the Kansas Leadership Center is one of an ongoing leadership intervention. We continue to struggle daily to live up to the ideals envisioned and set out at the Occidental Hotel back in 2007. Inspired by the audacious beliefs and acts of those early Kansans and the generosity of the Kansas Health Foundation that made KLC possible, the work done that day and the hard work done by so many thereafter gave rise to a set of guiding principles and competencies: a framework for KLC itself that is relevant to leadership in any setting. In the next two chapters, we share the concepts and ideas of key leadership thinkers that shaped our way of thinking and our understanding of the nature of civic challenges. Our hope and intention is that this framework will inspire you to become more deeply engaged in exercising civic leadership for the common good and will provide a guide for its practice.

Chapter 2

Thinking About Civic Leadership

It is easy to forget that a mere three centuries ago much of this country's population — native, immigrant, enslaved — had little control over the circumstances that shaped their lives and had no notion that influencing these circumstances would ever be within reach. These "immutable" conditions left many living impoverished, hardscrabble lives. The revolutionary ideas emerging from the European Enlightenment in the 16th and 17th centuries led to profound changes in economics, politics, education, medicine, science and technology. America's own revolution was rooted in these ideas. New thinking coupled with concerted action could and would change for the better the conditions in which people lived. Leadership — acting with intent to change life's circumstances for the better — was the engine that drove these transformations. Making progress relied on conscious and intentional action from those who cared enough to act.

In a book promoting leadership in the fractious and noisy civic context of contemporary America, it makes sense to settle on a definition of civics. If asked, the majority of people might characterize it as the interaction of citizens with government, focused on government oversight and operation. But we embrace an emerging understanding that broadens this description beyond government to include the role of ordinary citizens and others in the organization and workings of society to address common concerns. Embedded in this enlarged understanding is the notion that each of us shares directly in both the problems and opportunities of civic life, so we bear some responsibility for making progress.

As the conception of what *civics* meant expanded, so too did the understanding of what it would take to make progress in this challenging arena. In the 1960s, Peter Drucker, one of the 20th century's great management thinkers, spoke often about the importance of civic life, asserting for example that to be legitimate, management had to be "responsible for the social impact of its enterprise."[4] The reigning interpretation of civic leadership at the time held that this responsibility could best be fulfilled through social and volunteer work from those at the highest levels of the social hierarchy rather than through ordinary citizens themselves. Those at the top organization levels could be part of an elite, guiding force for civic life. Although not explicit, this interpretation often meant that a few influential and — hopefully — public-minded white men could and should decide what was best for the rest of us.

These were powerful men, at least within their own towns and regions, who knew other powerful men. They were men who thought they knew what needed to be done and went about doing it. For them, this meant doing things *for* others, without consultation, without engagement. In this way, the right things could be accomplished and the wrong things avoided, all without the turmoil and bother of a more inclusive and democratic civic culture.

Today, after decades of unrest and social change, this limiting conception of civic leadership no longer serves. No one has the authority or influence to tell anyone else what to do unilaterally, and the complexity of the issues strains our capacity to comprehend how we might make progress. Our present-day multicultural society, with its diverse and cacophonous factions, further complicates attempts to gain agreement, and the current polarizing and divisive civic culture undermines efforts to work out differences in ways that better reflect the common good. Tracing the history of the great social movements that so dramatically changed civic life along with the evolution of thinking about leadership provide a deeper understanding of the rationale for the Kansas Leadership Center's work.

In the 1960s and early 1970s, four great social movements came of age, changing the civic landscape in manifestly different and clearly visible ways that carried profound implications for civic engagement and civic leadership. These provocative movements — civil rights, grassroots, environmental, and women's — threatened traditional power structures, radicalized and mobilized unheard or disenfranchised voices and, at times, menaced the country with anarchy when institutions failed to change quickly enough. Each movement, with its own long, challenging and sometimes tragic history, seemed to mature and converge at roughly the same moment.

Years of protest and active resistance to racial segregation, primarily in the south, propelled civil rights to the forefront of American minds. The daily drama of televised beatings, fire hoses turned on protesters and dogs tearing into marchers heightened the tension. For many, the August 28, 1963, March on Washington symbolized the resolute power of the movement. Martin Luther King's defining "I Have a Dream" speech, designed "to arouse the conscience of the nation," set in motion a legislative trail that culminated in the Civil Rights Act of 1964 and the Voting Rights Act of 1965. These actions brought African-Americans and other minorities closer to full participation in civic life and eroded the power of one race to control the lives of another.

Saul Alinsky opened his 1971 book *Rules for Radicals* with this paragraph: "What follows is for those who want to change the world from what it is to what they believe it should be. *The Prince* was written by Machiavelli for the Haves on how to hold power. *Rules for Radicals* is written for the Have-Nots on how to take it away."[5] No anarchist, Alinsky wanted to work at the margins of the political system by organizing unheard voices to challenge those at the center. With no shortage of poverty-stricken workers and families, angry protesters of the Vietnam War, civil rights activists and disillusioned children of the middle class, Alinsky tapped into this latent energy to openly defy authority, assert needs, and demand change. Organizing the multitudes at the grassroots level could effectively challenge the traditional power of position, money and influence. Events such as the student strike at Columbia University in 1968, which ultimately forced the university to open communications to respond to students' demands, played out across the nation. This newfound capacity to organize and act helped grassroots or community organizers put the issues of housing, economic development and health care for the poor on the table. By creating advocacy groups around countless concerns, activists stymied the capacity of one part of society to act unilaterally. Alinsky's work continues to shape community organizing to this day, as evidenced by Tea Party activists using his principles to help organize their local campaigns.

Environmental activist and writer Paul Hawken describes the environmental movement as the largest social movement in the world.[6] It was not always so. Before the 1960s and the publication of Rachel Carson's powerful critique of the impact of industrial pesticides on the environment, *Silent Spring*,[7] environmentalism was the bailiwick of an elite and educated few who either cared enough or could afford to think about humanity's impact on the natural world. Her book democratized the movement, paving the way for powerful advocates such as The Sierra Club and The Wilderness Society to push these concerns to the foreground of public life. Now squarely on the agenda, these issues gained broader support from the masses while at the same time alienating many in the world of business and politics. No longer could influential industrialists or governments disconnect, without notice or protest, the interests of their institutions from the broader interests of citizens and the country.

Social revolutions ebb and flow. After great successes, causes often lie dormant awaiting renewed energy and action. And so it was with the women's movement. The actions of the first wave — the suffragettes of the 19th and early 20th centuries — gained the right to vote for women in 1920. Despite this substantial success, a woman's place remained in the home in most American minds. Even World War II's demand for industrial workers to be replaced by women, as "Rosie the Riveter," failed to provide much impetus. The postwar desire of returning soldiers for peace, good jobs, simpler times and comfortable lives at home squelched the ambitions of many women enticed by their WW II experiences. In 1963, Betty Friedan's book, *The Feminine Mystique,*[8] churned up the waters again. The book, with more than 3 million copies in print by 1966, described the discomforting and unsatisfactory circumstances of women's lives. The only way out, as many saw it, was to undermine the patriarchal myths about women's roles that closed them in. Since then, the women's movement has acquired new dimensions encompassing workplace rights, such as freedom from sexual harassment and a desire for equal pay for equal work, along with a much more expansive view of sexuality and power. Once again, a social movement had changed lives for the better while expanding America's civic and political landscape.

These movements have irrevocably redefined for the better who should be included in American civic life and the concerns that provide its focus. Many more people with a stake in public problems now demand a say in the political decision-making process and a place on the public's agenda for their concerns. By challenging the common, prevailing understanding through resistance and confrontation, these movements also created new demands and unexpected consequences. For one thing, newly empowered participants in civic life undermined the leadership capacities of the "city fathers." No longer could a small group of mostly white males on their own initiative chart the course of their communities and regions. Some people look back with nostalgia on these "simpler" times, lamenting the loss of control and ability to act. Others celebrate the possibility of a broader base of community members taking on the responsibility for leadership. Few understand what it takes to get something done in this civic world turned upside-down.

The notion of leadership is a curious one and deserves exploration if one is truly to grasp the nature of what KLC is working toward. At its most elemental, leadership entails one person influencing others to do his or her bidding. This raises a number of provocative questions. How does one do this, and why would others follow? What is the magic that allows some people to be effective when others are not? What and whose ends should leadership serve? Is leadership an activity or a position? How does authority differ from leadership and what kinds of challenges are best addressed by each? Do different contexts — for example, political, organizational and civic — demand different approaches to leadership?

These are not questions with easy, self-evident answers. Leadership scholars struggled with these questions just as KLC did in its early years. Tracing the evolution of contemporary thinking about leadership helped the team answer these questions and begin to characterize the Center's guiding theory.

Prior to World War II, few people seriously pondered such questions. Biographers wrote about great men as leaders while business experts conflated the term *leader* with that of *manager*, but no one looked at leadership itself as a concept to be studied. The war's vast mobilization of men and women for the military and industry raised questions about setting direction and motivating people, thus seeding the beginnings of this field of study. With millions of people at work and at war, understanding leadership became crucial. Then, in the postwar years because of the mass of data available on industrial and military performance, the study of leadership took off. Further enriching the field, psychologists working with social issues in communities and businesses struggling with employee performance problems fueled experiments in group dynamics and leadership.

Until the study of leadership developed some legitimacy and the great social movements of the 1960s and 70s created multiple centers of influence and power, two pervasive ideas constrained thinking about the subject. First, the untested assumption that leadership capacity was narrowly, not widely, distributed in the population excluded most people from the role. The thinking was that leaders are born, not made. This self-serving notion helped those in "leadership" positions justify and protect their roles. Second, the conflation of leadership with authority meant that the leader or an elite few could decide what should be done. That thinking went, through inspiration, persuasion or by somehow compelling people to achieve specific ends, the leader leads and followers follow.

Refuting these traditional defining ideas, broad spectrums of historically excluded peoples — African-Americans and women, for example — took up the mantle of leadership to address their own needs. The capacity to act was no longer concentrated in the hands of a few at the top levels of the country's organizations and institutions. It became clear that making progress in any arena — business, political, nonprofit or civic — would require new conceptions of leadership distinct from authority and position.

With changes fomenting in the decades before, 1978 marked the maturation of leadership as a field of study. In that year, political scientist James MacGregor Burns published his seminal work *Leadership*,[9] a difficult-to-read study that had far greater influence than Burns had anticipated. It defined leadership as a field of knowledge and a phenomenon that could be analyzed and studied: in doing so, Burns brought focus and direction to this nascent field.

He also raised the ante about what leadership could and should mean by distinguishing two fundamentally different kinds of leadership: *transactional* and *transforming*. According to Burns, a *transactional* leader engages followers in exchange for something valued, such as money, status or votes, but this exchange does not bind "leaders and followers together in a mutual and continuing pursuit of a higher purpose."[10] He contrasted this with *transforming* leadership in which the interaction of "leaders and followers raise one another to higher levels of motivation and morality."[11] The two types are not mutually exclusive. Transforming leadership may accomplish all the ends sought by transactional leadership, yet go beyond to inspire, to elevate, and to define goals constituting a renewal of social vision. This delineation of aspirations set the tone for the future of leadership studies and helped distinguish the field from management. Not coincidentally, Burns' work mirrored and described the transforming experiences of millions in the great social movements of the time.

In his Pulitzer Prize–winning biography of Franklin Delano Roosevelt, *Roosevelt: The Lion and Fox,* Burns explored that president's Machiavellian tactics, later saying in an interview, "He was a manipulator, and at the same time he had to be a lion. To what extent did he use the tactics of a fox in order to advance the wishes of a lion? To what extent did he have to be a transactional leader to be able to become a transforming leader?"[12] This predicament — balancing the immediately practical with a transcendent purpose or vision — remains the central dilemma for anyone interested in exercising civic leadership.

From questioning why some people succeed in leadership while others languish, Burns also probed the origins of leadership. Grounding his work in Lawrence Kohlberg's theory of moral development and Abraham Maslow's hierarchy of human needs, he hypothesized that "it is in the congruence of the levels of need ... and of the stages of moral development that leadership is animated, politicized, and enlivened with moral purpose."[13] He wrote that leadership development paralleled human development: a person grew through developmental experiences that might call forth a drive to exercise leadership. The further a person progressed through these developmental stages, the more likely the capacity to exercise leadership would be to emerge.

Burns' thinking on leadership development coincided with the exponential growth of the human potential movement. Human beings, in this view, had the "potential both for individual self-realization and for civic virtue . . . for an almost indefinite expansion and realization of people's human and generous possibilities,"[14] a premise that led to a fundamental rethinking of assumptions about how to develop these attributes. Humans could and would continue to develop throughout their lives; learning was not confined to youth and adolescence. Because personal development provides the foundation for leadership development, an individual's personal development and leadership capacities could be enhanced by participation in structured programs. Effective programs use a balance of experiential, cognitive and reflective learning processes to engage the whole person by integrating physical, emotional, social, mental and spiritual aspects and focus on learning processes rather than task completion, content knowledge or skills. If social responsibility and civic virtue were inherent aspects of leadership, the task of teaching others to lead implicitly carried these same expectations.

Burns' ambitious vision of what leadership could be and his disciplined study of this phenomenon brought rigor to a loosely defined and amorphous field. After Burns, leadership would no longer be subsumed in the study of management or viewed narrowly through the lens of epic biographies of great men. His insistent focus on the transcendent dimensions of leadership legitimized its study and established a normative dimension that had been lacking. Burns' work paved the way for leadership development organizations, including KLC, that aspired to his transformative vision.

It is hard to imagine a thriving KLC without the work of Mary Parker Follett. Nearly a century ago, Follett, a New England political scientist, anticipated today's civic challenges in her audacious critique of American democracy, *The New State.*[15] Writing in a time when few people used the words *leader* or *leadership,* Follett foreshadowed contemporary thinking on these ideas, defining power as "simply the ability to make things happen, to be a causal agent, to initiate change."[16] Going further, she distinguished "power over," the coercive power or influence of one person or group over another, from "power with," the synergistic potential of joint action. She argued that working together in a deliberative way to bring out differences creates the possibility of a deeper, more integrated response that goes beyond the limitations of compromise and concession. She understood that "power with" required a more consultative or facilitative style of energizing others to be effective.

Follett, who was no ivory tower political philosopher, no doubt would have felt at home at KLC. Steeped in the tradition of New England town hall meetings, she saw deeply democratic local action as the root of better politics. Without glamorizing localism — she understood the limitations of a narrow parochialism — she struggled to make American democracy more inclusive and participatory. Her own rough-and-tumble experience with small, deliberative groups — social centers, as she called them — in Boston's poor Roxbury neighborhood taught her the hard realities of this work. Often set up in public schools, these social centers provided a place where citizens could come together each week to take up local challenges and find practical ways to address them. Citizens were encouraged to do the work themselves rather than relying on social workers. The meetings were designed to bring out differences in a give-and-take process that acknowledged and preserved a diversity of individual ideas and insights and change them through interaction to create more unified responses and synergistic action.

In a country grounded in rugged individualism, these deliberative practices didn't come naturally. Follett recognized the need for "people learning how to evolve collective ideas."[17] "We must deliberately train for citizenship as for music, art or trade."[18] Through the various forms of local civic engagement she created, Follett used deliberation and group activities to stimulate development of the skills for working together and the motivation to act for the good of the community. These pioneering forums for civic leadership development set the stage for a deeper evolution of community leadership programs decades later.

A half-century after Mary Parker Follett, John W. Gardner came to similar conclusions about the need for widespread civic engagement. Gardner, whose career in public service began during World War II and lasted until his death at 89 in 2002, served six presidents in various roles, including Secretary of Health, Education, and Welfare under Lyndon Johnson. He also started Independent Sector and Common Cause and, in his last years, chaired the board of the National Civic League. He put his remarkable reflective powers to work writing nine books on public service and leadership and, as one of America's great public philosophers, inspiring countless Americans to action in civic life.

Gardner understood from his experience that if the nation were to make progress on its toughest problems, leadership would have to pervade all segments of society and that it would have to be a profoundly different kind of leadership than traditionally practiced. The challenges were too complex and the interests too diverse and conflicting for top-down leadership to be effective. The civic culture — the norms and practices of civic life — was too divisive and too reliant on government as the driving force. Few people acted across factional boundaries or spoke reliably about common interests.

Because of these conditions, he said, "We must develop networks of leaders who accept some measure of responsibility for the society's shared concerns. Call them *networks of responsibility,* leaders of disparate or conflicting interests who undertake to act together on behalf of the shared concerns of the community or nation."[19] The key to civic progress, in Gardner's mind, was to transform the default civic culture from a "war of the parts against the whole"[20] to an inclusive, engaging and collaborative one that could make communities better for all. To do this required building relationships, skills for working together, and a sense of responsibility for the future of the community or region. Broad access to powerful civic leadership development experiences in America's communities and regions could speed this transformation.

In the 1980s and 90s, several keen observers of American civic life, John Parr, Bill Potapchuk, Neil Peirce and Curtis Johnson noticed that some communities were making notably more progress on civic challenges than others. While not yet the norm, civic engagement was at the heart of these successes. Two aspects characterized these more successful communities. First, a few civic-minded people recognized that the default civic culture — the "war of the parts against the whole" — hindered progress. Second, they made conscious choices to do something different, convincing others that more progress could be made by working across factions rather than against each other. By serving as conveners, catalysts and facilitators of these initiatives, these people were learning how to exercise leadership in an inclusive and collaborative way.

"The table gets larger and rounder,"[21] wrote civic journalists Peirce and Johnson in *Boundary Crossers: Community Leadership in a Global Age;* "the agenda gets tougher"[22] and "no one's excused."[23] Working across factions and engaging unusual voices had become a way of life in some places, even if it was messy and frustrating.[24] Not coincidentally, those places making the most progress also were reaping the benefits of years of investment in community leadership development. Mary Parker Follett's vision was coming alive.

Leadership, according to leadership guru Warren Bennis, a contemporary of Gardner and Burns, "in its simplest form is a tripod — a leader or leaders, followers, and a common goal they want to achieve."[25] This narrow assessment captures the conceptual orthodoxy accepted and developed in most leadership writing and research. In this view, leadership implicitly resides in an individual in a distinctly hierarchical relationship with followers, a narrow conception that helped sustain the belief in the exclusive rarity of leadership capacity and the conflation of leadership with authority. Burns, too, operated out of this paradigm, defining leadership as "leaders inducing followers to act for certain goals."[26]

But another, more dynamic way of looking at leadership, mirrored in the practice of KLC's philosophy, is to view it as an activity or process that energizes or mobilizes others to make progress. By detaching leadership from position and authority, one opens the possibility that each of us has the opportunity to exercise leadership at any time in any situation. This democratizing notion is both liberating, because each of us has the capacity to lead if we so choose, and demanding, because each of us then shares responsibility for making progress. "Followers" can no longer defer to or blame those designated as "leaders" for lack of progress.

Rural Kansas has been fertile ground for more than wheat and cattle. Back when Wesley Hospital served the citizens of Wichita, Kenneth Benne, a graduate of Kansas State University in 1930, began his long career in education as a schoolteacher in Concordia and Manhattan. Rooted in this experience and with a subsequent Ph.D. from Columbia University's Teachers College, Benne helped develop the field of social foundations of education by analyzing the relationship between education and social contexts. During World War II, Benne connected with psychologists Kurt Lewin and Ron Lippitt and fellow educator Lee Bradford, who were researching military morale and psychological warfare. After Lewin died in 1947 and inspired by him, Benne, Lippitt and Bradford started the National Training Laboratory, an institute that produced fascinating and influential insights into organizational development and leadership.

Lewin and Lippitt already understood how different approaches to leadership could dramatically affect the behavior of a group. In the early 1940s, experimenting with small groups of young men, they found that laissez-faire leadership led to cynicism and authoritarian leadership led to obedience or infighting, while democratic leadership led to tolerance, less selfishness and more conscientious behavior. They also noted that when a group's leader changed to someone with a different style — say, a democratic leader replaced an authoritarian one — the group quickly began to reflect that style. One obvious implication was that if one could increase mastery of different leadership styles, one could become more effective in a wider range of situations. Much of the subsequent work on situational leadership built on these observations. Less obviously, this research signaled a step toward understanding leadership as an activity or process rather than a position or authority.

The Connecticut Workshop, run by Benne, Lewin, Lippitt and Bradford in 1946, pushed the learning deeper. Operating on the premise that "You cannot know an institution until you try to change it, and you cannot change it without reflecting on its purpose,"[27] the four didn't hesitate when asked to intervene in a tense situation in Bridgeport, Connecticut. Fifty participants from many walks of life — teachers, social workers, business people, community organizers, union members, housewives and even a few gang members — came together for two weeks to work out some of the city's ethnic and racial tensions in a group setting. Using role-playing, small group discussion, and a three-part process Lewin called "unfreezing," "learning" and "refreezing," group members confronted their biases and fears. "Unfreezing" allowed a person to shed old beliefs, "learning" provided new ideas and approaches and "refreezing" solidified new behaviors.[28] As the work progressed, Lewin and his partners noted the dynamics of the group and observed how participants had changed through the experience. One of the more reticent members of the group, a social worker named Mrs. Brown who became "a very active and verbal leader"[29] through the process, caught their attention in particular. Looking back on and evaluating what they had witnessed, Lewin and his partners concluded that participants in groups like these (they called them T-Groups) could learn and dramatically change by reflecting on their behaviors in the group and experimentally applying what they had learned in subsequent group activities. It was also clear, as exemplified by Mrs. Brown, that leadership in these leaderless groups was not dependent on one's position or authority. Anyone in the group could exercise leadership at any time if he or she wanted to. The work of Lewin, Lippit, the Connecticut Workshop — and Mrs. Brown — further informed and was seminal to KLC's thinking.

Several decades later, Harvard Business School professor John Kotter staked out new ground surrounding the purpose and activity of leadership. Referring to leadership as "a process that helps direct and mobilize people," he distinguished it from "a group of people in formal positions where leadership … is expected."[30] He went on to note the confusion caused by the second definition because "it subtly suggests that everyone in a leadership position actually provides leadership" when this is obviously not the case.[31]

An effective process of leadership produces movement. Leadership is a "force for change," unlike management, which must produce predictable, orderly results.[32] "The function implicit in this belief is *constructive* or *adaptive change*"[33] and is achieved by attending to three tasks or sub-processes: establishing direction by developing a vision, aligning people to cooperate to achieve the vision and motivating and inspiring people to keep moving toward the vision. By explicitly focusing on purposeful change and the processes required to bring it about, Kotter took another step toward understanding leadership as an *activity* rather than a position or authority.

Perhaps the most trenchant contribution to the unraveling of leadership orthodoxy and the development of KLC's philosophy came from an unlikely source, psychiatrist Ron Heifetz. Picking up on Kotter's thread that leadership is a force for change, Heifetz recognized its inherently conflictual nature. Political, organizational and civic challenges are adaptive by nature. Their complexity demands new and unorthodox responses to make progress; the status quo simply will not do. To change existing circumstances, one must confront them. This means confronting all the attachments people and organizations have to their own ways of seeing the world, and changing these views entails loss of identity, status or other valued aspects of one's life. Few people, it seems, are willing to undermine their own identity without immense provocation.

Heifetz's background clearly shaped his understanding of leadership. As a psychiatrist, he was trained to provide expertise by diagnosing a patient's condition and prescribing a way forward. On the other hand, psychological issues generally resist such technical solutions and require the patient to do work of an adaptive nature to make progress. These challenges are complex and systemic, meaning that routinely treating a symptom is unlikely to address the root cause. He may be able to provide some observations about the patient's condition, make some inferences about the cause and provide some advice about how to face painful circumstances and develop new attitudes or behaviors, but for real progress to be made, the patient must do this work. Just as the psychiatrist mobilizes the patient to do work, leadership must mobilize others to do work. In this sense, anyone with the gumption to act can lead. As Heifetz and Riley Sinder write, "There is no such thing as 'seizing leadership,' since leadership is not a position but an activity."[34]

Creating useful change in a world of fragile human beings with hypersensitive egos is no easy task. These are psychological challenges, and Heifetz insists they be seen as such. To create change requires intervention: an activity. For that activity to be effective, one would have to appreciate and consider these psychological dimensions before and as one acts. Intervening is an experimental and improvisational art with no guaranteed outcome; indeed, the activity of leadership begins with a personal intervention from anyone with the courage to act.

Most contemporary students of leadership acknowledge that it can be learned in carefully designed programs in which powerful teaching interventions impel participants into transforming experiences. These experiences can help a person come to terms with the risks and benefits of exercising leadership while building up courage to intervene or act. They can also help participants become more purposeful, conscious and intentional, thus more effective, in their practice of leadership.

Not surprisingly, from Heifetz' perspective, the most challenging obstacles to becoming more effective at exercising leadership are psychological. Embedded in a person's psyche or ego, largely automatic and unconscious responses constrain how one acts or reacts in a given situation. Heifetz calls these responses defaults that can be reset by increasing awareness of them and cultivating a wider range of responses. Through a careful diagnosis of one's capabilities and the nature and demands of a particular situation, a person can more effectively respond to make progress.

In the last 25 years, Heifetz and his Harvard Kennedy School partner, Marty Linsky, pioneered a powerful pedagogy — later adopted by KLC — capable of challenging and expanding these default settings even with those most resistant to change (curiously enough, often those with the most success in authority roles). Starting from the premise that all of the raw material needed to learn about leadership is alive and well in any group, their case-in-point method seeks to use the immediate experiences of individuals and the group to help participants learn about leadership. The dynamics of a group in the classroom — competition, authority, power, deference, dominance and so on — mimic both the challenges and the opportunities for exercising leadership in communities and organizations. Through the case-in-point approach, Heifetz and Linsky help participants confront the gap between their aspirations and their own, often feeble, attempts to achieve them. This is difficult and disturbing work for most participants because it forces them to acknowledge how much their behavior — their part of the mess, as Heifetz and Linsky called it — contributes to the lack of progress on the issues they care about. Confronting habitual and comfortable behaviors in this way often leaves participants disoriented as they attempt to digest and integrate these experiences. It takes moxie to do this taxing work with others. Case-in-point teaching helps others recognize how fraught leadership is with both the strengths and frailties of human beings. Learning to cope with these aspects in an experiential way helps people learn what it takes to realize their highest aspirations in a world of conflicting interests and competing values where difficult choices have to be made.

This much is plain: exercising leadership — either within or beyond one's scope of authority — is inherently risky. The risks are both personal and professional. Self-esteem and reputation are both at stake, and once a person intervenes, he or she loses significant control of the outcome. The willingness to risk depends on how much one cares about making progress on the presenting concern and one's tolerance for the ambiguity of an uncertain outcome. Confronting personal psychological obstacles that impede learning and progress requires an openness and courage few people possess. Learning from the mistakes that will occur can be more difficult as well as more fruitful than understanding successes. These are daunting challenges, and it's not hard to imagine why so few people are willing to exercise leadership on the concerns they say they care about.

The rewards are perhaps less apparent but equally motivating in the writings of Follett, Burns, Gardner, Heifetz and Linsky. All recognize the hazards and the difficult, even excruciating work of exercising leadership, yet each provides the inspiration for pursuing it. In their own way, each expresses the passion and thrill of personally exercising leadership as a way of bringing meaning and purpose to their lives. The mission and programs of KLC build on and extend these ideas.

The coming of age of the great social movements expanded and transformed the civic landscape. The convergence of these events and thinkers set the stage in Kansas for a promising social experiment: Could civic leadership help build healthier communities? Could civic leadership development at an unprecedented scale transform the civic culture of a state? The Kansas Health Foundation thought so, and in January 2007, the Kansas Leadership Center began its work.

Chapter 3
The Adaptive Nature of Civic Challenges

Once we had identified the state's major problems in our 2007 listening tour, we began to understand and distinguish them as *adaptive* or *technical* challenges, a concept pioneered by Ron Heifetz and Marty Linsky. Though we'd read and appreciated their work over the years, crafting a framework for distinguishing messy, complicated adaptive problems from the more clear-cut technical ones hadn't been in our minds. When Ed attended the week-long Art and Practice of Leadership Development program at Harvard's John F. Kennedy School of Government in 2007, he began to realize that Heifetz' and Linsky's approach to describing challenges would be helpful for our work in civic life.

Already well aware that building a consensus around an approach to leadership would be challenging and that the severity of the issues facing Kansans was extreme, distinguishing the adaptive versus the technical elements of the work offered a way to understand an inherent duality in civic life. On the one hand, civic entities are fully capable of solving many incredibly complex problems — a county can create and run a system for real estate valuation for thousands of properties annually; school districts can develop systems to track student performance and teacher evaluations; a transportation agency can design and build massive freeway systems with complicated interchanges; a nonprofit can raise millions of dollars and provide backpacks of food to hungry school children; advocacy groups for low-income citizens can devise complex, yet effective, incentive programs to encourage savings and asset-building. Clearly, technical problems such as these are being identified and addressed in the civic sector.

On the other hand, successful implementation of complicated initiatives seldom helps make progress on the myriad related but messier and much more complicated adaptive challenges. Although educators can track student performance, teachers, parents, proponents of school renewal and other advocates are far from agreeing on what the scores mean and how they can be legitimately used to prescribe actions that would arrest a troubling decline. A government agency can design and build a multilevel highway interchange, but it has few workable ideas on how to get its citizens to be less reliant on their cars and interested in more sustainable transportation. A nonprofit may be able to help a few low-income individuals rise out of poverty, but it is hard-pressed to create sufficient systems and momentum to address inequality on a larger scale.

It's not that talented, competent and committed individuals aren't working to improve communities everywhere; without question, they are. The problem is that the type of leadership necessary to organize and manage a freeway project isn't the same as the leadership needed to promote long-term transportation sustainability. Likewise, what it takes to mobilize donors and volunteers needed to put food in backpacks for hungry kids looks much different from the leadership necessary to combat poverty and hunger across an entire population.

This illustrates the familiar and age-old dichotomy of treating symptoms rather than causes. Comedian Jon Stewart made the point in late 2010, when he joked about how eight presidents in succession, from Nixon to Obama, have publicly announced a plan to rid the United States of its dependence on foreign oil. He showed video clips of the eight men making sincere declarations of intent and presenting ideas for alternative energy sources, timelines and a definition of success. Nixon wanted to eliminate all foreign sources of oil for the country's energy needs by 1980, while George W. Bush wanted to reduce foreign oil consumption by 75% by 2025. Following the clips, Stewart deadpanned, "We have redefined success and still failed!" He summed it up, saying, "Fool me once, shame on you. Fool me twice, shame on me. Fool me eight times, am I a [freaking] idiot!"

For our purposes, *idiot* is too strong a word, but *conspirator* sounds about right. The truth is that issues such as reducing oil dependence and consumption exemplify the ever-present, seemingly overwhelming adaptive challenges confronting our communities, regions, states and nation at every turn. The unfortunate reality is that, through neglect, denial or apathy, all of us conspire to avoid working on these kinds of challenges, allowing them to grow and become even more daunting. In the end, they go unattended because few of us have the leadership skill and necessary drive to face and doggedly pursue them. Directly addressing these sorts of adaptive challenges takes a kind of leadership seldom exercised and rarely rewarded in the civic arena.

The effective exercise of civic leadership requires an understanding of the difference between adaptive and technical challenges. The work of Heifetz and Linsky is especially helpful in making this distinction. They identify six requirements for making progress on adaptive challenges:[35]

- Solutions lie outside our current way of operating.
- Solutions require learning.
- Solutions require a shift in responsibility from authority to stakeholders.
- Solutions require distinguishing what is precious and expendable.

- Solutions demand experimentation.
- Solutions require longer timeframes than we are accustomed to.

Whether it's a nonprofit organization, a city, a state or a nation trying to improve education, grow the economy, help vulnerable populations or crack the code to fiscal reform, all six requirements pertain.

A quick look at one aspect of the health care debate illustrates these dimensions. Traditionally, medical care focuses on treatment rather than prevention. Prevention requires new knowledge, attitudes and practice; that is, it takes learning about and experimenting with new approaches to determine what works. Each of us — stakeholders — must take more responsibility for our own health and learn to eat better and exercise more, thus helping prevent health problems. These behavioral changes take time. Treatment alone will not improve health.

As our early work at KLC evolved, we recognized that progress on technical problems comes through good management, appropriate expertise, workable plans and efficient execution. It was also clear to us that Heifetz and Linsky's requirements for making progress on adaptive challenges called for a different, more provocative and engaging kind of leadership. Based on the months of interaction and thinking about what we wanted to achieve and the roundtable planning discussions that followed, five guiding principles and four competencies ultimately emerged to form the framework for the Center. We had, indeed, begun to define a different approach to civic leadership, one that informs and supports the work we do to this day.

Those guiding principles state that leadership is an activity, not a position; that anyone can lead anytime, anywhere; that leading starts with one's self and then moves on to engaging others; that clarity of purpose is essential; and that leadership is risky. The competencies, behaviors directly related to the principles and discussed in greater depth in succeeding chapters, include *Diagnose Situation, Manage Self, Intervene Skillfully* and *Energize Others.*

Working in concert, the four competencies help turn the practice of civic leadership for the common good into a reflective and intentional pursuit. Two of them, *Manage Self* and *Diagnose Situation,* are contemplative and diagnostic in nature and provide a deeper understanding of self and one's context to help guide the activity of leadership. The other two, the action-oriented competencies of *Intervene Skillfully* and *Energize Others,* bring leadership to life by mobilizing others to act. Employing those competencies, though not always easy in practice, often makes the difference between successful and unsuccessful civic leadership.

It soon became apparent to our team that, without exception, every one of the six requirements of adaptive work, along with each of our own principles and four competencies, directly applied to our own organization. We grasped how essential it was for us to practice what we believed and would be teaching; we knew we would need to keep learning and experimenting, give the work back to all participants and make the tough choices about what in our organization would be precious and should continue, as well as about what would impede progress and should be dropped. And, recognizing from the outset that our mission of transforming the civic culture of a state would require decades to accomplish, we committed to the work for the long haul.

It was not lost on us then, nor have we forgotten since, that the continuing development of the Kansas Leadership Center is itself an ongoing adaptive challenge.

While this book offers a different, more effective approach to civic leadership, at the same time it is also a book that tells stories — a number of them. The first was the tale of Kansas' early days followed by how the Kansas Health Foundation came to be and how that led directly to the creation of the Kansas Leadership Center. The academic, professional and personal accounts of those who influenced the field of leadership bring us to the present juncture.

As we developed the four competencies, drawing on existing leadership theories and, more importantly, what we heard from Kansans, we began to see them appear time and time again. The stories of individual Kansans whom we knew had exercised civic leadership on tough adaptive challenges long before KLC began gave us confidence that our framing was close to the mark. We recognized that these examples might be useful in helping others learn how to address their own civic leadership challenges.

As we go forward, then, we'll tell the stories of real-life, contemporary characters, five people active in five different aspects of civic life, each passionately engaged in and wrestling with an adaptive challenge. We've chosen these particular individuals because of the variety, breadth and critically proactive nature of their civic experiences: a former Speaker of the Kansas House of Representatives, a nonprofit executive director, a mayor, a pastor and a community-minded emergency medicine doctor.

Although each of these people had some level of formal authority, the extent of their influence was limited. As Heifetz notes, the responsibility for making progress on adaptive challenges must shift from those with authority to stakeholders. In many ways, these exemplars were what we have come to call the *usual* voices who learned how to exercise leadership differently to bring overlooked or excluded *unusual* voices into the conversation. The inspiring aspect of their leadership was their willingness to risk acting far beyond the constraining boundaries of their authority roles to facilitate this shift.

In each circumstance, as in any leadership situation, the reader will note the enormous amounts of work involved and the positive steps taken along with missteps, questionable calls and outright failures. Whether one agrees with all the actions taken or not, there are lessons to be learned from these players and their situations. To us, each individual is deserving of admiration for simply, to use Theodore Roosevelt's words, being "in the arena ... for a worthy cause."[36]

In the unfolding of the stories of our exemplars, we will introduce and illustrate in the next chapters KLC's four competencies of civic leadership in a way that conveys the nonlinear, iterative, interactive and systemic nature of our concepts in real-life practice. At the end of these chapters, we will go into the deeper dimensions of the competency with an eye toward advancing your own capacity to learn to lead. By providing some contemplative questions, we hope to stimulate your own learning and development. We will especially focus on contrasting defaults — those habitual, often unconscious ways of reacting or responding — with alternative possibilities for expanding your repertoire of potential leadership responses so you can be more effective in a wider range of situations.

Each of the five stories focuses on a central adaptive civic challenge, but by no means should this suggest that is the only challenge, adaptive or technical, the individual faced. It would certainly be much easier for all of us if problems arose one at a time without becoming enmeshed in other concerns or issues, but life doesn't work that way. For all of us, challenges of all shapes and sizes abound that must be addressed. It was no different for our exemplars.

Doug Mays

Conservative Republican Doug Mays enjoyed a long career in public service. We'll meet him during his second stint as Speaker of the Kansas House of Representatives when he guided a legislative body with an overwhelming Republican majority. Managing a legislative body is never easy, and a number of challenges weighed on the man with the top job.

True to the characteristics of adaptive challenges, no precedent existed for how to achieve health care reform in the state; no one knew how to go about the task. The prospect of figuring out how to tackle such a complicated issue as well as provide leadership in what would no doubt be an extremely contentious process seemed nearly overwhelming given all of his other responsibilities. Navigating this complicated terrain would pose an adaptive challenge Mays would come to know well. His story illustrates the care he took in managing himself.

Lance Carrithers

Pastor Lance Carrithers recognized that thanks to the steady influx of immigrant families in Dodge City, the changing demographics would eventually affect his church. At First United Methodist, as well as in other mainline churches in the community, he'd noticed both a decline in membership and an inability to attract Hispanic members. As he began to connect the two issues intellectually, he felt called to build a growing community of people of faith regardless of their race.

In his diagnosis of the situation, Carrithers would encounter a number of adaptive challenges and, in accepting that the path ahead would be neither simple nor easy, he was determined do what needed to be done to make the changes he believed were necessary.

David Toland

Born and raised in Iola, Kansas, David Toland embodies the classic profile of the small-town boy who goes off to the big city and returns home to do good. The University of Kansas graduate, a fourth-generation Jayhawk, went to Washington, D.C., where he worked as a top assistant to the mayor. His post-Iola life took him far, literally and figuratively, from his southeast Kansas roots. But when a local foundation offered him a job to head its ambitious plan for improving the health of Allen County, Kansas through community revitalization, Toland accepted. He and his family returned to live in his hometown, and Thrive Allen County had its first executive director. There may be no better example of an adaptive challenge than the nebulous idea of "community revitalization." With limited resources and almost no formal authority, the stark challenge of energizing residents throughout the county to create profound changes in health policies and behaviors would prove neither a simple nor an easy task for Toland.

Laura McConwell

Laura McConwell, a University of Missouri at Kansas City–educated attorney who practices law with her father, is also the sitting mayor of the Kansas City suburb of Mission. As mayor of a town that is still vibrant but has aging streets and bridges coupled with declining housing and commercial stock, one of McConwell's ongoing challenges was to improve and maintain these aspects of the city's infrastructure. To do this, she and others in the city would have to raise and apportion revenues from city taxes and other monetary sources to cover the increasing costs. But there was no easy solution to Mission's funding dilemmas, a situation shared by many other deteriorating American suburbs. One hallmark of an adaptive challenge is that it requires new ways of operating or intervening, and McConwell set out to identify and implement a novel approach to addressing these problems in her hometown.

Denise Dowd

Traditionally, hospitals care for the sick rather than engage communities in prevention work. Because there's no quick fix to the nebulous challenge of violence prevention beyond deterrence by the possibility of heavy, post-incident legal penalties, Denise Dowd, pediatric emergency medicine physician, found herself faced with the embodiment of an adaptive challenge on any number of levels. The story of her efforts over a span of years portrays the course of an individual who finds she must diagnose a situation and intervene skillfully to energize others around her, all the while learning to manage herself.

In recounting the stories of our five exemplars, our intent is to present and illustrate the various dimensions of the competencies through the lens of their individual approaches to real-life adaptive challenges. In each of these accounts, as happens in all such leadership situations, actions and reactions get muddled, leaving ample space for differing interpretations of whether the individuals made progress or not. There are no black-and-white successes or failures here. Instead, many shades of grey and a host of colorful characters illustrate how civic leadership can and should be at once more purposeful, engaging and provocative.

Part II

The Practice of Civic Leadership

Chapter 4
Manage Self

One of the greatest obstacles to exercising effective leadership can be our own ego. For some of us, the desire to have all the answers or control the outcomes and be seen as all powerful blinds us to the realities of the situation. For others, the fear of being disliked, discounted, dismissed or disrespected undermines our courage to act. Visceral emotional reactions such as anger or grief hamper our ability to assess the situation and respond effectively. Being aware of these tendencies, vulnerabilities and triggers while cultivating other, possibly uncomfortable, ways of responding can help us deploy our abilities in more productive ways.

As individuals, human beings often have an extraordinarily hard time with change, even when it is imperative and eminently sensible. Collectively, it seems we are part of a larger social system that tends toward inertia. The pressure to maintain the status quo is immense. A current situation, no matter how crazy it may be or how obvious the course of action might seem, serves someone's interests either through maintaining existing advantages or by avoiding prospective losses. Any change to the status quo knocks the system out of balance, with no good way of gauging the outcome.

As an example, take the situation of Denise Dowd, the pediatric emergency medicine physician we introduced earlier in Chapter 3 and whose story we will come back to in Chapter 8. Her professional education provided the knowledge and expertise needed by a physician to diagnose accurately and treat medical problems. And, as a doctor, she was used to some level of formal authority in her work with others. The system in which she worked imposed tremendous expectations on her to assess a medical emergency quickly and begin treating it immediately. Nurses, physician assistants and other aides deferred to her authority. Within this narrow context, she had both control and status and, over time, developed a perhaps overrated sense of her own importance. As she became more concerned with violence prevention, an adaptive challenge much less amenable to expertise and authority, the loss of immediate control took a toll on her sense of who she was, her ego. It took several years for her to realize she would have to let go of her reliance on expertise and authority and her own self-importance to learn better ways of exercising leadership and make progress.

We all have preferences — defaults — in how we respond to the pressure to act or react; sometimes we're conscious of these, but more often we are not. For many of us, these preferences are emotional and reactive rather than rational and intentional, as with Dr. Dowd's various "reliances" noted above. To exercise leadership effectively, we must overcome these internal and external obstacles. Whether one is engaged in a small, personal matter or in a larger one playing out on the public stage, competently managing ourselves takes personal awareness, the capacity for realistic — even ruthless — assessment of strengths and weaknesses and a willingness to experiment with new and possibly uncomfortable ways of leading in challenging situations.

Now consider the quite public situation facing Doug Mays back in 2005. Celebration of the beginning of his second term as Speaker of the Kansas House of Representatives was cut short when, foreshadowing the coming national debate and actions on health care, Governor Kathleen Sebelius issued an Executive Reorganization Order creating a new Division of Health Policy and Finance. That new executive-branch division would manage health insurance for state employees, oversee the state's Medicaid program and, the governor hoped, expand health insurance coverage for low-income Kansans and provide coverage subsidies to small businesses.

Although most people considered Sebelius to be a collaborative governor, her executive order drew a mixed reaction. And, as often happens with such orders from any governor, her action brought an immediate response from across the aisle. Along with other Republicans, Speaker Mays was taken aback by her action and felt the executive order was unnecessary. He, in particular, was angry about it — spitting mad, some would say. To him, what she'd done usurped the responsibility of the legislature, and he vowed he wasn't going to stand for it. From his earliest days in politics, the observance of governmental separation of powers had been of supreme importance to him, and now, in response to this action, he determined to make sure that the state's legislative branch would have its say.

To say that Mays had a temper was an understatement. He was well aware of his fiery temper; controlling it had been a lifelong challenge. After serving 10 years in the House and now a two-year term as Speaker, he knew firsthand that conflict was inherent in politics, and, in his role, he'd come to understand that managing conflict — with others and within himself — was one of the great challenges of his position. But for him, managing his own anger — in this case, his primary default reaction — mirrored what he had to do in the House, and the one presented just as great a challenge as the other. He knew that allowing himself to give in and get angry, especially when the stakes were as high as they were in that case, only made things that much worse. So, exercising all the fortitude he could muster and reminding himself that there may have been one or two times when he'd tried to do something similar, he was able to ride out the shock and throttle back his anger. That he anticipated the political conflict *and* his own anger likely made all the difference in the eventual outcome.

Mays' political instincts told him that rather than flat-out kill the thing, as he wanted to do and might have done had he not been able to check his default reaction so successfully, the Republicans needed to find a viable alternative. Thanks to having his anger under control, Mays took a step back, calmly looked at the issue, and was able to appraise what was being proposed. Then, from that same calmer vantage point, he asked himself to assess the governor's idea honestly; if it was a good one, he believed he could help find a way for Republicans to embrace it.

Successfully managing oneself requires both a thorough diagnosis of the situation and an accurate assessment of one's own strengths and vulnerabilities. At other times in Mays' career, things might have turned out differently. If he hadn't been aware of how much influence he carried in his role as Speaker and how others had seen him react in the past, left uncontrolled, that quick-to-flare anger might have circumvented any attempt to construct a viable alternative and deepened an already existing antagonism and mistrust between the legislature and the governor.

As it turned out, Mays determined that Sebelius' plan had significant merit. To acknowledge the positive aspects but avoid saying "no" out of hand to the executive order, Republicans built on the governor's plan and proposed creating a new Health Policy Authority. After working through a series of compromises about the structure and purpose of the entity, which included the additional responsibility of advising the legislature about innovative approaches to health policy, the legislature passed a bill establishing the Kansas Health Policy Authority (KHPA), which Governor Sebelius signed into law in the spring of 2005.

Working the health care reform initiative through the legislative process was only one of many challenges in those years that tested Mays' leadership skills. And right in tandem with those challenges was his ever-present need to manage his self-acknowledged problematic personal defaults. In an arena characterized by conflicting values and behind-the-scenes intrigue, political and personal acumen count far more than real authority. He knew and accepted that other than the formal procedural rules a Speaker had for controlling the agenda and workload of the House of Representatives, the person in his position had little control over outcomes. He understood and embraced the knowledge that his role was to set the agenda, work with all the parties who wanted to be involved, and serve as a facilitator of the process.

Although quick to anger, as he will tell you, Mays is also thoughtful, one who tries hard to keep the bigger picture in view. He'd long felt that as the foundation for serving in the Kansas Legislature, it was most important for him to have broad knowledge of what was going on in general, a good feel for the specific issues and an equally good feel for what the public wanted, as well as what would best serve the state: a good place to start for almost anyone who finds him or herself in any position of leadership. In the case of the health care legislation, thanks to Mays' reasoned appraisal of the situation and his attendant self-management, he was able to do his part to help prevent a potentially damaging conflict likely to end with nothing accomplished for the citizens of Kansas.

As effective as Mays was in this instance, while casting back over his career, he readily admits there were many other times when he, as he put it, "got in his own way." At those times, he acknowledges, he was not so successful at leading. He will also tell you that by nature he is a results- rather than a process-oriented individual, which meant that as Speaker he sometimes overlooked parts of the process and inadvertently left out people who should have been included.

As it was for Mays, then, and as it is for anyone exercising leadership, personal awareness was a key element in managing self. Besides being aware of himself personally, another factor contributed to his success in the political arena: his awareness of how others perceived his role or his politics and then deftly using that understanding to help make progress. By the time the health care reform negotiations were underway, Mays, who'd been in politics a long time, was heavily identified with the Republican Party and recognized as much more conservative than the governor. While he enjoyed a good relationship with the state's top executive, instead of taking point on that project, he asked Senate President Steve Morris, whose relationship with Sebelius was even better, to act as point person. The old pro Mays knew if he could get the right people in the room from both parties and from the governor's office, some good work could be done. He was right.

One might think that anyone who wanted to be Speaker of the Kansas House would have a certain amount of hubris; belying this notion, interestingly, Mays' own feelings of inadequacy, another default, were ever-present. He worried, and continually attempted to squelch the worry, that people would "figure out what an idiot [he was]." His way of controlling his fears of inadequacy, which stand as good advice for others in leadership situations, was to listen and absorb what was going on before speaking or acting. In the Statehouse, he was able to gather himself while listening as others talked and things got pretty heated on the floor — or, as was more tellingly the case, "screaming and stamping" or "reacting with a flood of negative emotion." Having remained quiet throughout those tempestuous exchanges, when the storm had played itself out, he would judiciously use the limited authority of his role as Speaker to keep the process moving. As a rule, in the House chamber he didn't often get up to offer his view, but waited until everyone had his or her say. Then, when he did speak, people knew it was important to listen.

Other aspects of managing himself as Speaker meant that Mays, who was continually having to choose among competing values and requests, had to weigh his own preferences or desired outcomes against the pragmatic imperative to get something done. He also knew his actions were under greater scrutiny than those of other legislators and that, by virtue of where he sat, what he said or did would have greater consequences. To walk such a tightrope, he knew he needed help and advice from others, people who would reliably check his interpretations of what was going on and report their honest opinions, telling him outright if they thought he was right or wrong. This meant that to resist seeing things narrowly through his own default perspectives, to manage himself, it was crucial that he cultivate a well-grounded, impartial group of people who had a good idea of what all parties were thinking. In his particular case, as Speaker he also needed people he could trust who weren't going to pander to him. He well understood that in a position such as his, a person is often so busy that there isn't as much interaction with the greater body or organization as a whole. Always after taking the bigger-picture assessment of any situation, he was less interested in the political leanings of those who would report to him than in their character, valuing their judgment and honesty over adherence to the party line.

What emerges from the story of Mays' years of leadership is the profile of an insightful, pragmatic individual, one who came to better know and then manage himself. No easy tasks, those, but necessary, and since he was more than willing to do the hard work in any number of areas to look for, and find, ways to bring people together to make things work, he found success at many turns. And so it is for any who step up to engage in the activity of leadership; build on Socrates' injunction to know yourself and, we would add, then use that knowledge in managing yourself.

Lance Carrithers, pastor of Dodge City's First United Methodist Church, faced a much different situation than Doug Mays, although he, too, practiced self-management in addressing what became, for him, a central adaptive challenge. Rather than herding cats in the state legislature, Carrithers wanted to corral his traditionally white congregation within his inclusive vision of a multicultural, multiethnic church. For him, this was the embodiment of the Christian recognition that all people are God's children. This work entailed challenging some widely held assumptions about how to go about engaging in ministry to Latinos. From the start, it was not the easiest of paths for this particular pastor, a naturally engaging and likable man for whom, he acknowledged to himself and us, being liked is especially important. He found he would need to confront his congregation with what would most likely be for them an uncomfortable interpretation while managing in himself his dominant desire to be liked by others.

Preternaturally sociable and not a bit hesitant to speak his mind about what led him to this aspiration, Carrithers' actions exhibit one of the hallmarks of self-management in not having been afraid to examine his own prejudices, his own sinfulness and to call them into question. He went about this mindfully, looking into and judging his own life and views as much as he tried to call out the sinfulness or the prejudices of his congregation.

In this instance, to get the ball rolling, he stood up before his congregation one Sunday morning and told them, in language as direct as he could make it, about his childhood growing up in the small community of Johnson in the 1960s and the countless times he hadn't given a thought to the brown-skinned people who also lived there. He confessed how completely ignorant he'd been of their real, daily lives and their suffering. Such a confession was important, he believed, because he wanted to make sure his listeners knew that he'd stood where they might well be standing that day, that he was not judging anyone without first having judged himself. He continued, explaining that, although he was in no way proud of it, his complete lack of awareness of the real nature of the lives of those hometown neighbors allowed him to believe none of it was any of his concern.

Looking out into the faces of his congregation, he saw that they were listening to him with interest and even curiosity, and, no denying it, a measure of confusion. In more than a few of those faces he read wonder at where in the world he was going with the long yarn he was spinning. He'd certainly shared personal anecdotes before in illustrating points he wanted to make, but nothing this drawn out. He pressed on, saying the realization of that lack of awareness of his brown-skinned neighbors then became a central tenet of his examination of his own need to change, giving that last word a punch. "I saw it was what I absolutely had to do." And in that change, he told them, he was referring to the kind of preacher he never wanted to be — the person who stood before his flock, shaking a finger and telling them they were all sinners and had to do things differently. There in the pews before him, his congregants sat wide-eyed listening to him, and in that moment he knew he had them.

His sense had been that any initiative to bring Hispanics into a predominately white congregation would undoubtedly bring competing values into play, and Carrithers believed that challenging the implicit hypocrisy of the situation — his desire to live out the deepest values of Christianity versus a conservative congregation's desire to worship with others like themselves — would significantly raise the cool, complacent temperature in his church and open up the possibility that some longtime members might well leave. Those were risks he was willing to take.

Carrithers was well aware that his Christian faith and the time spent in prayer to seek discernment and strength helped him weigh these competing values. His belief was that this kind of work cannot be sustained without the strength one gains from one's own personal spiritual discipline or practice. In some ways echoing Doug Mays, he described his role as one that names and identifies what an issue is, what is out there as part of "the brokenness in the world that is not the world as it might be or could be by God's grace."

Now, as Carrithers will tell you, for most good pastors impatience comes with the calling, and sometimes this personal attribute caused him to rush to judgment and outpace the people he served, as happened with moving his congregation to being more open to Hispanic people of faith. A related personal default surfaces in the blinders to external information that often piggybacks onto his impatience when he feels driven to accomplish something. After his Sunday sermon, when he'd laid out the story of his early life in Johnson and his ignorant dismissal of so many of the people who lived and worked there, he knew that a healthy number of his listeners were with him. The handshakes were hearty that morning, the thanks plentiful; he felt he was well on his way. That's when he drew on the blinders for a bit and got to planning, assuming those shaking his hand and thanking him for the good sermon would fall into step with him immediately and that his vision would soon and easily become reality. It didn't work that way, and he had to tap the brakes, slow down, and let people catch up with him. To this day, he still works hard to counter that tendency.

Carrithers' approach to mobilizing his congregation — talking to them about himself and his own path — was an intuitive one; he hadn't participated in a KLC program, so he wasn't familiar with its concepts or terminology. He later observed that both the approach and the intuition underlying it were the products of who he was and where he came from. Whether inherent or learned, his ability to see the world as it ought to be, know it's not like that and then move others to act represents strong aspects of self-management in the service of more effective leadership. But to this day his greatest weakness, he knows and freely admits, is that ever-present, nearly overpowering desire to be liked. Extroverted and operationally perceptive, his desire to have people like him continues to hold him back from acting when he should and too often causes him to crumble in the face of confrontation. On his best days, thanks to his well-honed process of self-coaching, he's able to manage himself without becoming paralyzed in the face of all the attendant troublesome feelings.

Carrithers understood that to make progress on the controversial issue he cared so deeply about and the adaptive challenge he wanted his congregants to take on with him, he would have to act in ways that were uncomfortable to him, countering his desire to be liked, in order to raise the troubling issues. His own self-management, he knew, was critical in even beginning the process, much less in gaining a successful outcome.

David Toland had a different internal struggle to contend with. Unlike Carrithers, he had never been overly concerned about how much others liked him; instead, his quick intelligence and assertiveness sometimes outran his sensitivity to others.

Smart, well-educated, self-contained and in his mid-30s, Toland returned to living in his childhood Kansas hometown of Iola to invest himself in a very big job — turning around Allen County's perennial status as one of state's least healthy regions. One might be excused for thinking that he, with his University of Kansas undergraduate degree in political science and public administration and six years of experience as a Deputy Chief Operating Officer in Washington, D.C., Mayor Anthony Williams' administration, had taken a step down in accepting the position of director of a two-year-old grassroots coalition, Thrive Allen County (TAC). While he certainly didn't see it that way, what had ultimately clinched his decision to accept the job was the opportunity to come home with his wife and raise a family in what they believed would be a more wholesome environment than the nation's capital.

Though he'd been gone from Allen County for a number of years, his parents and other family members had remained and, thanks to visits home and an abiding interest in home-state doings, Toland felt he had a good grasp of what he was getting into. He knew there was no question that local politics in Allen County would be much different from the heavy-handed power plays he'd experienced in Washington. For one thing, in the close-knit towns of Allen County, he knew the citizens and communities could ill afford the collateral damage of a roughshod, win-or-lose approach to the critical issues facing them; in no way would the take-no-prisoners politics of the big city be the order of the day. He also knew he could not come in with his usual "know-it-all" approach. From his early days one of his acknowledged tendencies, which we would term a default, was to quickly dismiss the views of others in the belief that he knew the right things to do. Through the years, that tendency has proved a mixed blessing for him. Because he was often right and adept at seeing things through to a good end, he'd enjoyed some success; on the flip side, the out-of-hand dismissals of others' views had occasionally gotten him in trouble.

In the weeks before the move, reflecting on his return to Kansas and without anyone pointing it out, he knew those old, ingrained traits of his wouldn't go down well in a sparsely populated rural Kansas county where outsiders were roundly distrusted. He figured he'd be building on the limited credibility he had as a Kansas native son and known quantity, the latter thanks to his well-known parents and grandparents. Or maybe because, he thought — or hoped — some of them might remember him as a likeable Iola kid. Whatever social capital he thought he had, he was determined to spend it, and he hoped to do so wisely.

Given to offering colorful metaphors, Toland sometimes characterizes his approach to work in military terms, seeing himself as a general who takes charge, addresses a particular situation, works hard on it, accomplishes the stated outcome and then marches on to the next thing. As a student and, later, in his high-stakes D.C. job, this take-charge-and-get-it-done default had been his successful working model, and he figured it would serve him well in his new job. But in those days of contemplation before actually taking up the work, what he failed to account for was the possible downside to being that way, and soon enough he saw that it could run counter to the real and essential need in Allen County to encourage hundreds of people to share responsibility for their health. Indeed, what he found early on was that others involved in seeing to the organization's work seemed to key into that default by playing to his presumed authority as an East Coast expert. Almost immediately, the board began to step away with, what seemed to him, a collective sigh of relief and the feeling of "Okay, we've got our guy and he's got the know-how. Let him go, let him figure it out." Aware of the usual drive and intensity of his general's personality already in play, he came to fear that their acceding so wholeheartedly to him in his role as CEO would only exacerbate his natural tendencies. These were real and reasonable concerns. Soon he understood that if he were going to make a difference, he'd have to keep tight control of himself, keeping his own defaults in check. The tendency that he'd honed in his past work proved to be a double-edged sword there in Allen County — good for him in many situations but not necessarily in all. This is true of defaults any of us may have; a clear strength in one situation might well prove to be a vulnerability in another. It's all the more reason to be conscious of them and aware of how we manage them.

As Toland was getting settled in his job and back in the community, it soon became apparent that others in Allen

County had less noble views of him. Some of the talk went that he was "the mouthpiece" for tax-hiking liberals in the community and that he'd been hired to further their liberal agenda. Another and perhaps more widely held view was that he'd taken the job with unstated political aspirations, as a stepping stone toward something else in Kansas or elsewhere. Aware of the various, though not necessarily apt, perceptions of him, Toland used this insight to help him build on positive aspects and counter the negative ones as he begin his work. Sometimes, he recognized, he'd need others to take the lead when his motivations or credibility might come into question. Over time, he felt his actions and his persistence would provide a corrective to the differing perceptions.

Much in the way we did in the early days of KLC, before jumping in, Toland toured Allen County, listening to and talking with residents in all its towns. People spoke to him about health, theirs and their community's in general, and what they thought needed to be done. He listened to a man's story of having to travel too many miles to wait hours and hours to be seen in an emergency room for what amounted to routine care. He listened as a woman explained how she was sure her family members' problems with being overweight would be helped if only they had a newer car and could get to a gym. The story of a young couple that still didn't understand why or how their two-month-old baby had died nearly brought him to tears as they talked. The stories troubled him, and often saddened him. He listened to the many suggestions floated by people for improving the county's poor-health plight. Many of the ideas were good ones, and some were potentially workable, but some of them were clearly outside the range of his and the board's conception of the coalition's role and purpose. He quickly came to understand the impossibility of trying to be all things to all people.

Part of the problem, Toland recognized, was that when people unloaded their ideas on him, they believed he would become a partner in them. But it would be impossible for him to be a partner in everyone's dream or vision, no matter how worthy or how much he might want to do so. Toland knew that he already had and would continue to deeply disappoint a number of people. Personally, he had to work to accept that reality. A difficult but necessary part of managing self is the capacity to choose among competing values. He had to be judicious in choosing his battles while keeping all relationships as open and productive as he could or risk squandering the meager resources and good will available to transform Allen County's poor state of health.

Doug Mays knew he needed the help of trusted individuals to help him manage himself in his role as Speaker. So, too, did David Toland understand that he needed allies as he waded into the deep waters of his adaptive challenge in Allen County. Even with that in mind, his headstrong nature often led him to jump to conclusions about the motivations and positions of others. One situation in particular, one whose stakes were high for him and that could have cost him dearly, is one that can serve as a reminder to all in a similar circumstance. To lobby support for an initiative to build a new hospital, members of the TAC team went out to talk with people in the community about the project and solicit their backing. Toland was advised that a certain community member was thought to be an adversary to their plan whose support was unwinnable; agreeing, he accepted the opinion and wrote that individual off the list. But then one of his advisers suggested he talk to the written-off person to verify the accuracy of the interpretation, and so, warily, feeling as if he were on a fool's errand and would likely be thrown out of the office, he requested a meeting. The depth of his surprise when he was graciously greeted could not match what he felt when the individual told him that, while not enthusiastically supportive of the initiative, he was certainly not opposed to it. Toland realized his instincts in the matter — his having jumped to yet another know-it-all conclusion — were completely wrong. But rather than castigate himself for his incorrect appraisal of the individual, he felt a measure of pride in having put aside his assumptions to listen to the counsel of another, as well as a measure of pride in being courageous enough to have done something he truly dreaded. Because he successfully managed that know-it-all default, the outcome was a win-win situation.

Coming from the political turmoil in Washington, D.C., Toland was used to conflict, yet he was surprised by the discord and sometimes outright hostility in Allen County. Taking the job and accepting the challenge, he'd hoped to be in a position from which he could effect change by leading efforts, and he hoped to have a platform from which to espouse his vision for a healthier county. And that's exactly what he got, though it was more contentious than he envisioned it would be. Whether in the nation's capital or in a small rural county in Kansas, he's still living with the conflict inherent in adaptive work, and he's had to work particularly hard to manage himself every step along the way.

Toland's natural drive and intensity have taken a toll on him. His friends, fearing burnout, counseled him to slow down and not take on so much. But his response is that he doesn't intend to spend 20 years in the job, so it's okay for him to maintain his pace and purpose. His work also strained his family life. His parents worry about the controversy that goes with his role, and he and his wife worry about what might happen if things don't go well. He acknowledges the risk, saying it's "riskier than anything we've ever done." Ironically, in an organization focused on health and well being, Toland may be an early casualty unless he can learn how to find a better balance between his professional and private lives. To succeed, in the long run, he will have to learn how to take care of himself.

Mission Mayor Laura McConwell faced a less ambiguous situation than David Toland or Lance Carrithers. At least she thought so; the problem she wanted to address — developing the city's physical infrastructure to escape the crumbling fate of so many inner-ring suburbs — appeared to have more clarity. But her efforts took an unexpected turn one spring when she was pushing forward a novel method to fund these improvements. The use of this new method — one that had been used only a few times in other places — might help her avoid a dreaded and always unpopular increase in property taxes. It was something closer to a user fee, based on the reasoning that those who used the streets should help pay for them.

The idea for this proposed Transportation Utility Fee (TUF) received praise from some for its innovation as an alternative to a property tax, but it also ignited a widespread civic firestorm. When talk radio joined in, picking up the idea as a topic for on-air discussion, it stirred up opposition from anti-tax advocates and other naysayers. The so-called "driveway tax" debate was full-on in Mission, landing McConwell in the middle of a battle she hadn't anticipated and one that would mightily test her capacity to manage herself and stay the course to try to get something accomplished in the city.

The no-nonsense, straight-shooting mayor jumped directly into the fray by actively engaging people on all sides of the issue. Because McConwell appreciates hearing other opinions and believes everyone should participate in the process, controversy and disagreement are things she'd never shied away from; in this instance, ultra-heated though it became, her attitude was no different. She recognized that, as mayor, she would be an easy target for anger and criticism of the issue and understood the futility of trying to fight the more emotional reactions from some of her opponents. Discounting those emotions or feelings, she knew, would only escalate things and make the situation worse. Besides, she reasoned, even with people who just wanted to throw stones — and there did seem to be a fair number of those — there was nearly always something worthwhile to think about in what they said. Few of us want others to be upset or angry with us, and in that McConwell is certainly no different, but as long as she believed in the greater truth and benefit of her position in the matter of this initiative, she didn't let others' opinions and hard feelings keep her up at night. Echoing Doug Mays' approach, McConwell kept in mind the bigger picture for her city. And, in her case, her default response — openness to hearing and crediting the views of others — was a help.

Not everyone was against the initiative; many in the community, along with the city council members and staff, saw things as she did concerning the non-property-tax approach to addressing the crumbling infrastructure. These people, she knew, looked to her to stay strong and hold the course. They all believed quite sincerely, given what was known from community surveys and an earlier, in-depth visioning process, that most residents were supportive of what she and the council were doing. The streets desperately needed fixing, and she needed to take a stand on it. If she didn't, she thought, losing legitimacy with the larger community would be far worse than kowtowing to the naysayers.

Although McConwell had the right strengths to follow through, paradoxically, a weakness that she felt sometimes got in her way — what we would categorize as a default — was letting everyone have his or her say when some things she was responsible for simply didn't need much dialogue. In the midst of the community flap over the proposed "driveway tax," she set up a public discussion session at the Mission Theatre, a sort of town-hall meeting, hoping to clarify what the proposal was all about and, she also hoped, quell some of the uproar and begin to bring the community closer to consensus on the issue. Thanks to that default and her wanting everyone to have his or her say, things pretty quickly got out of hand at the meeting. A free-for-all wouldn't be far from an apt description of what went on in that old theatre that evening, with people venting their heated opinions of both the proposal and the mayor. It was clear that many saw her as part of an evil empire designed to beat the little man. Others took her for a punching bag and slugged away. She knew she was an easy person for them to fuss and holler at and say awful things to. And probably many thought that the meaner and nastier they got, the more likely she would relent and change course.

But she was able to remain calm and, in response, to try to cool things down she went back to the beginning and attempted to explain what she and the city were doing, what the purpose of the meeting was, and what they had done in advance of the vote. It was no fun at all, but she knew that as mayor she had to be there doing what she was doing. Perhaps, though, had she been more aware of and able to manage that problematic default, things might not have reached the blazing level of discourse they did that night in the Mission Theatre.

As mayor, one of McConwell's strengths was her capacity to distinguish what it took to set a direction and decide what to do from what it took to implement the decisions. Getting to a decision requires engagement. Implementing a decision requires staying the course. And although some people may have seen McConwell as ruthless, her capacity to manage herself when the heat was up helped Mission make progress on its chronic problems of deteriorating transportation infrastructure and on escaping the fate of so many metro-area suburbs.

Manage Self is one of the four civic leadership competencies that inform and reinforce each other, enhancing our capacity to lead effectively. Learning to manage ourselves helps us become more aware of our defaults and preferences while developing a wider range of responses to challenging situations. This self-knowledge allows us to counter our own resistance to change and to be more conscious and intentional about how we exercise leadership.

As illustrated by these four people in quite different situations, *Manage Self* manifests in unique ways dictated by circumstance and personality. Laura McConwell, for instance, made the most of her ability to hold steady to move vision to action. Lance Carrithers had to overcome one of his vulnerabilities — his desire to be liked — and act outside his comfort zone to bring himself and his congregation face-to-face with discrimination in his church community. The discipline of his spiritual practice helped him discern the competing values at play and make conscious choices among them. David Toland's understanding of the stories others told about him tempered his tendency to assume he knew what needed to be done and act impetuously. This allowed him to engage others more effectively on an issue that, to make progress, required widespread changes in behavior. In the rough-and-tumble politics of the Kansas legislature, Doug Mays knew his own anger could, in an instant, undermine his credibility and influence as Speaker. But when events such as Governor Sebelius' independent actions in the health reform saga triggered his anger, the Speaker kept tight control of his temper. This control and his strong relationships with others in both parties allowed him to play a productive role in creating a bipartisan alternative.

Each of these Kansans had to become accustomed to the uncertainty and conflict inherent in adaptive work while courageously choosing among competing values to make progress. Without the capacity to Manage Self, the activity of leadership becomes reactive rather than conscious and intentional. With self-knowledge comes self-efficacy.

Manage Self

Exercising civic leadership effectively requires knowing yourself well enough to recognize how appropriately positioned you are to intervene. On the one hand, this competency involves self-diagnosis in a candid, even ruthless way and, on the other hand, making clear-eyed, conscious choices about how you deploy yourself in a given situation. To do this, you'll have to challenge your beliefs and assumptions about your own strengths and limitations and expand the repertoire of possible behaviors and approaches you use to exercise leadership.

- **Know your strengths, vulnerabilities and triggers**
  - Each of us has both strengths and limitations. What is it about you that either helps or hinders your capacity to mobilize others?
  - In a given situation, what can others do or say that triggers emotional reactions in you — either positive or negative — that may interfere with your ability to exercise leadership?

- **Know the story others tell about you**
  - Each of us has a story or belief about who we think we are. Others may see us in quite a different light. What is the story that others, especially potential adversaries, believe about you? What stories about who you are and how you exercise leadership are especially hard for you to consider?
  - In a particular situation, what is the story others tell about you and your motivations to exercise leadership? Consider multiple perspectives.

- **Choose among competing values**
  - Exercising civic leadership requires choosing among oft-competing values such as work, family, religious beliefs, financial security and the common good. What can you do to consciously weigh these competing values to help assess the risks of civic leadership?
  - In a given situation, what are you willing to put at risk in order to make progress on what you say you care about?

- **Get used to uncertainty and conflict**
  - Conflict and uncertainty are inherent in any context, none more so than in civic life. What about you either helps or hinders your ability to tolerate or cope with conflict and uncertainty?
  - In a given situation, what makes exercising leadership difficult for you?

- **Experiment beyond your comfort zone**
  - Expanding your repertoire of leadership responses takes experimentation. What are the uncomfortable behaviors, interventions or actions that might be needed from you to make progress on what you care about?
  - In a particular situation, what experiments might you undertake to expand your repertoire of leadership behaviors, interventions and actions?

- **Take care of yourself**
  - What part of you — physical, emotional, spiritual, psychological, relational, etc. — needs more attention if you're to be effective in exercising leadership?
  - What experiments might you undertake to attend to these needs?

Chapter 5

Diagnose Situation

Often we think we have a better understanding of a situation than we actually do. The human mind is capable of taking in extraordinary amounts of information, though frequently those capabilities go untapped. This phenomenon is abundantly apparent when it comes to diagnosing a situation in the civic arena. Time and time again we quickly assume we know what we need to know and then, just as quickly, move to action.

The embattled former United States Secretary of Defense, Donald Rumsfeld, was on the receiving end of many jokes for his attempt to explain the challenges he faced when a situation required action. In 2003, *Slate Magazine* posted his comments about knowing what we know in the form of a poem:

The Unknown
As we know,
There are known knowns.
There are things we know we know.
We also know
There are known unknowns.
That is to say
We know there are some things
We do not know.
But there are also unknown unknowns,
The ones we don't know
We don't know.
Donald Rumsfeld, February 12, 2002,
Department of Defense news briefing

Politics aside, Rumsfeld was on to something. In leadership, when trying to understand — *diagnose* — a situation or issue, few people probe deeply enough to discover and interpret what is not readily apparent; the leadership challenge is to ensure that we understand as much as we can. Descending to this deeper level leads to many more questions than answers, and exploration for answers leads to a more complete and accurate understanding of the situation. This, then, helps us to intervene more skillfully.

It's hard to resist the impulse to jump to action and show progress quickly. Expectations from others can easily compel us to act without thinking things through. Many of us are trained as experts, to know what to do — *now* — which may be helpful with technical problems, but not with adaptive challenges. Because these conflicting pressures can force us into ill-conceived actions, the risk is high that we'll fail to understand the true complexity of a situation and the real barriers to progress, leading us to misdiagnose the situation.

We can look at diagnosing a situation on two levels: one having to do with what is apparent, the other with what is more profound. Most of us spend our time at the surface level, clarifying what we think we know and then reacting to these preconceptions using our expertise both to diagnose the problem and provide solutions. The phenomenon is not unlike the situation of a physician who uses an x-ray to diagnose a child's broken arm, then reduces the fracture and immobilizes it with a cast. This is clearly technical work — applying existing knowledge and expertise to resolve an obvious problem — perfectly appropriate for such circumstances. The primary leadership task, then,for addressing technical problems is simply to find reliable and trustworthy expertise to respond appropriately.

But adaptive challenges are vastly different in nature and call for a more penetrating analysis. These challenges demand new learning and understanding as well as shared responsibility for acting to address them. Adaptive situations require a heuristic approach: the way forward must be discovered through trial and error much as you would find a path through unexplored territory.

Furthering the medical analogy, let's consider a person with heart disease. The doctor may be able to diagnose the medical symptoms of the disease yet cannot fully appreciate its causes without engaging the patient in conversation to understand the behaviors that led to the current situation. The doctor may well be able to provide some relief through medical interventions or pharmacological responses, but in the larger frame of overall health the patient will, at some point, have to take responsibility for making lifestyle changes to improve health and fitness. As the work evolves, the patient's responsibility and role in improving his or her health will become more prominent. So it is in civic leadership. Without the active engagement of those who are both part of the problem and, therefore, part of the solution, little progress will be made.

The second, deeper level of diagnosis, then, requires distinguishing the technical and adaptive elements of the situation, identifying who is involved and who must do the work, discerning the level of conflict — or "heat" as we call it in KLC programs — and discovering the conflicting, perhaps unsettling interpretations of what's going on. Since responding to adaptive challenges demands that we engage others to make progress, we have to pay as much attention to how the work is done — the process — as we do to what the work entails — the content.

When trying to help an organization, community or state make progress on tough issues, it's critical to understand as fully as possible the situation one is dealing with. Take, for example, the Kansas Health Foundation's mandate to the Kansas Leadership Center — develop civic leadership to address the state's most pressing challenges — and the insistent expectations to act that came with it. Without the team's strong commitment to its early listening effort, an uncomfortable cocktail party encounter between Ed, the Center's CEO, and a sharply critical state official impatient with the perceived "slow start" of the organization might have ended in a significant setback or even failure for the fledgling enterprise. At that early stage, it would have been easy to give in to the pressure from that official or from a number of others. Rather than stay the course and design a curriculum to fit the specific Kansas context, KLC might have simply adopted an existing leadership development curriculum. This approach undoubtedly would have been less threatening to those in civic and political authority positions in the state and, perhaps, less risky for the Kansas Health Foundation. But it could not have developed the capacities necessary to achieve our deeper purpose — helping Kansans make progress on the civic concerns they care about. At that time, we didn't call our listening tour diagnosing the situation, but that was what we were doing. The tour helped us understand the challenges we would face in trying to transform the civic culture of a state. We knew we had to get beneath the surface of what was going on in Kansas to understand the melody beneath the words.

Getting to that deeper, second level of diagnosis and distinguishing the technical and adaptive elements of a challenge are essential for anyone interested in exercising effective civic leadership. Although he couldn't have put his finger on it at the time, Lance Carrithers' first big challenge upon taking over as pastor of First United Methodist Church in Dodge City would be to develop a better understanding of the church's fundamental culture.

Carrithers' new town, Dodge City, was familiar to him. He'd grown up in western Kansas but had spent the past 15 years at other churches in the eastern part of the state. Even so, he was well aware of the massive population growth stemming from immigration in the southwest region. Fueled by the meat-packing industry, Dodge City had become an attractive destination for immigrant workers, especially those from Mexico and Central America. Its Asian population was growing as well. A generally prosperous and historically significant town, Dodge City found itself faced with addressing this rising tide of immigration and fast becoming a majority-minority community.

The education system was the first major institution that had to change to accommodate the influx of immigrants. But whereas schools had been compelled to modify their teaching and learning environments to make room for languages other than English, the pace of change moved more slowly for most other public and civic institutions. Despite being a majority of the population in the city, few Hispanics held political office or served on boards of nonprofit or other civic organizations.

Carrithers had heard mostly positive stories about how well Dodge City's residents were getting along, leading him to assume that he'd find a friendly, thriving multicultural community upon his arrival. He had no reason to suspect otherwise until a surprising encounter on his first weekend in town quickly changed his rosy assessment.

To the lively sounds of forks clinking against plates and friendly waitresses offering more coffee to patrons, Carrithers and his wife were chatting, making plans and enjoying a quiet breakfast at a main-drag café when a group of men entered. The Carritherses nodded and smiled at the men as they passed by on their way to a neighboring table. But just a few moments later, what they heard coming from that nearby table had them looking at each other, wide-eyed and gape-mouthed in astonishment. Openly, loudly, the men were spewing some of the most hateful, disgusting invective they'd ever heard, every word of it directed toward the local immigrant community. The profanity and name-calling were shocking enough, but the evidence of bigotry and racism that so obviously drove it was truly horrifying to the pastor and his wife. He'd known some people weren't especially happy about the number of immigrants and the changes they'd brought to the community, but to hear those opinions expressed so blatantly and in such crude terms in a public place stunned him. He felt sickened.

That was Carrithers' introduction to a more disturbing interpretation of the impact of Dodge City's changing demographics, and it fostered the beginnings of his attempt to get a better handle on the situation. Coming to understand the adaptive nature of these multicultural challenges would prove critical to him, as well as to his church, in the years to come. At the time, although he didn't have the formal concept of adaptive challenges or the language of *Diagnose Situation* to guide him, Carrithers instinctively began initiating his own assessment of the situation by describing, interpreting and testing what he found.

Grounded, principled and comfortable enough in his skin to be able to talk openly even about his own not-so-sterling qualities, Carrithers knew in his heart that he and his church had to help the community address the changing cultural dynamics of their town. So, not long after that breakfast, he set out to get a better sense of just how inclusive his congregation was. He was encouraged to find that there had been sincere efforts to try to connect with the Hispanic community; for one thing, the church offered what was a well-intended technical solution to that more complex adaptive challenge, a weekly service given in both English and Spanish. While crediting this admirable effort to foster a link with the Hispanic community, he discovered that only a handful of Latino families attended the service and that they all spoke English. It was plain enough to him that this effort simply wasn't getting at the underlying cultural differences that kept the Hispanic community and First UMC's congregation apart. By taking a longer, deeper view of the situation, he recognized that, however well intentioned, the bilingual service didn't in fact serve the broader need. Within a year of Carrithers' arrival the services were discontinued. An ironic move, perhaps, but one made by distinguishing an unsuccessful technical approach to what he had come to understand was an adaptive challenge. And it had also become obvious that nothing more was likely to happen unless someone, most likely him, consciously acted to change the situation.

The pragmatic Carrithers recognized that his church's future, in terms of membership numbers, likely depended on bringing in new Hispanic members. He was also idealistic enough to believe that bridging this divide was what people of faith are called to do. In his heart he felt that if his church could authentically engage different cultures, it might set a precedent for the broader community. First United Methodist, after all, was a prominent and affluent church, its membership made up almost entirely of working professionals actively involved in the community's civic life. His instincts told him that to make progress, he would have to tailor his leadership efforts to his assessment of the church's situation, what at KLC we would term a *conflict-laden adaptive challenge.* Carrithers simply called it doing what needed to be done to do the right thing.

For starters, to get a true handle on where his congregation stood, to truly diagnose the greater situation, he needed more information. After much reflection and prayer, one Sunday morning Carrithers made a statement from the pulpit that surprised more than a few in the pews before him. Their church could not remain as it was, he told them. "If we do, there's a great likelihood we'll become half the church that we are." After letting that declaration settle in some, he went on to explain his view that, within the membership of their church, they had the opportunity to become more open to reflect the diversity of the community. Again he paused, letting his words hang in the air, and then finished by saying, "In which case we might become twice the church that we are."

The pastor's intent was to shake things up and, from the startled looks on the faces of his congregants, he saw that he had. He knew he was being provocative and that what he'd told them was an exaggeration, but he needed to get a read on his congregation and find out how much they cared about the issue. He wanted to know how sensitive they were, discover what buttons he'd be pushing by saying such a thing to them, and from it learn which members were sympathetic, which didn't care and which would react negatively to the provocation. If he were to push ahead, he needed to know who might be with him. It was a way, but perhaps a risky one, to collect information that could be used to help him decide what to do next. Articulating it in the way he did, in those words, Carrithers was probing for a diagnosis of the situation.

Reactions came quickly. Some people were confused by his assertion because, in essence, what he'd said was that the congregation couldn't sustain itself as "an affluent country-club church," a pejorative term he apologized for using when relating the story to us. Others wondered why they couldn't just be who they'd always been and do what they'd always done. And a few, he found, were angered, even incensed, by what he'd said. His actions and words had "put a burr under the saddle" that began to irritate people. Carrithers' willingness to gather more information and bring to the surface differing interpretations helped him more fully understand the situation and then make better choices about how and when to intervene. As an initial step, he was fully aware that he was, again in his words, using his "bully pulpit" to raise awareness by reminding his congregation of the moral values at play.

As Lance Carrithers' story illustrates, understanding implicit process challenges — those reflecting the barriers and difficulties one faces in working with and engaging others — contributes significantly to a successful diagnosis of a situation. From hurt feelings to long-standing prejudices, Carrithers faced a good many of those kinds of challenges in his various attempts to engage his congregation with Dodge City's Hispanic residents.

While pondering how to respond to Governor Sebelius' executive order reorganizing the state's health agencies, process challenges also cropped up at every turn for Doug Mays. If the

Speaker hadn't understood these, it's likely the Republicans would have failed to counter the governor's move. Some of those challenges included the governor's neglecting to reach out to both parties in the legislature to help formulate her idea, resulting in Republican animosity toward her and her staff after being excluded from the process; the subsequent building of a consensus within his own caucus about how to respond; the communication with the House's Democratic caucus and the Senate; and the acquisition of adequate information to inform the work. Mays also had to contend with the formalized process challenges inherent in a public, legislative body, such as open-meeting laws and parliamentary procedures. A surface-level diagnosis focusing on the dimensions of health care reform and how the state's agencies should be organized — the content of the issue — simply would not have been enough. The second, deeper level of diagnosis had to focus on process, the challenges that most worried Mays and what we have found most often trips up those engaged in exercising leadership.

For Mays to act, he needed to understand and interpret the different interests, motivations and actions taken by others; he needed to keep the bigger picture in view. For instance, the governor may have felt she had the political strength to decide what should be done, so she failed to see the process challenges she would face in dealing with the Republicans. Mays' initial reaction, that the executive order threatened the separation of powers, may merely have provided a rationale for masking the anger he and the other Republicans felt about being outmaneuvered. Had they continued to be triggered in this way, Mays and his colleagues might well have lost sight of the original issue of health care reform. Aspects of both of these interpretations were alive and well in the fraught circumstances following the governor's announcement. Exploring these tough, uncomfortable but realistic interpretations in the moment helped the Speaker and his colleagues develop the ideas that led to a better outcome for lawmakers and for the state.

As David Toland and the people involved in his organization learned through experience, diagnosing a situation is neither a one-time nor a single-level task; rather, like Doug Mays and Lance Carrithers — or anyone engaged in civic leadership — they were involved in a multidimensional, evolving situation, and the process of diagnosing it would have to be ongoing.

At the outset, Toland had well-documented information about Allen County's worsening health situation. The results of a 2009 study conducted by the Kansas Health Institute[37] clearly implied that the overall health of the county's residents would continue to decline unless powerful interventions and policies could move the trends in a positive direction. Thrive Allen County had been established to create just these kinds of interventions.

With the wealth of information about the county's health status providing a benchmark for measuring progress along with an existing organization and a strong, active board that had already established a good foundation for the work, one can imagine how tempting it might have been for an intelligent, well-educated man like Toland simply to ask experts in the health arena to analyze the situation and make recommendations about what should be done. At first glance, this approach might have seemed sufficient for a diagnosis. He then could have assumed, reasonably enough, that he knew what he needed to know and could move quickly to action. His job would have been simply to convince others that these technical responses would work.

In reality, that sort of first-level diagnosis could not have helped him distinguish the deeper, more complex adaptive elements of the challenges. He might have understood how the disturbing trends could have been improved, but this expert-driven assessment offered little insight into how he could energize others in the county who would have had to do much of the work. To successfully diagnose the situation at the deeper level it required, he would need to identify the various factions with differing points of view along with their interests and motivations, size up the conflicts and process challenges that prevented deeper engagement and then figure out who needed to do the work.

In some ways, David Toland didn't really know anything when he arrived. As others have done before him in similar circumstances, he soon determined that he needed to get out among the people the coalition would serve and learn how they perceived the situation. His listening tour, he hoped, would allow him to help calibrate the needs and expectations others had for TAC. Once out on the tour, it didn't take long for him to discover how contentious the situation was; more importantly, the tour helped him understand that a concern for health in the county was simply not part of the culture. What he discovered first-hand complicated the harsh realities of the raw data and highlighted the adaptive nature of the challenges. The data indicators portrayed a crisis, whereas his interviews uncovered a culture of complacency. This was a poor combination, he knew, for making progress unless he could create a sense of urgency — raise the heat, in KLC terms — that would motivate others to take on the work.

Based on this ongoing assessment, Thrive Allen County experimented with a range of actions for expanding the breadth of influence of the organization, each a response to the conditions at the time as Toland and his board understood them. Their multidimensional, ongoing process of diagnosing the situation helped them make conscious choices about how to proceed and built the foundation for more far-reaching and profound interventions.

Mission Mayor Laura McConwell learned about the importance of diagnosing the situation the hard way following a listening session after the city council approved the Transportation Utility Fee. She had assumed — a benign interpretation — that she knew what citizens wanted to do about the city's deteriorating streets. But the response from some of the city's residents to the proposed TUF, which would pay for the improvements, surprised her and the city administrator. A visioning session earlier in her administration had tapped into the good will of participants but had failed to provide a glimpse of the troubles they would encounter when moving to action. McConwell proceeded with the implementation of the fee with little consideration for how others might view it. Soon enough, she would find out more about these differing and uncomfortable interpretations.

Her tendency to view most of the city's challenges as technical problems that could be addressed by the city's staff sometimes kept her from seeing the adaptive elements of those value-laden issues. As her story illustrates, recognizing the differences based on an incomplete understanding is not always easy, let alone using this understanding to suggest ways she might act differently. Her single-minded focus on purpose helped her hold steady in high-heat situations, but it also led her into conflicts that might have been prevented if she'd had a deeper appreciation of others' perspectives. Had she taken sufficient time to identify the different factions and tease out the differing interpretations of what was going on, events might have gone much more smoothly for everyone. These diagnostic insights could have provided the basis for preemptive actions or for creating a more effective and trustworthy process for engaging others. Absent an adequate diagnosis of the situation, these kinds of anticipatory and skillful actions are hard to imagine.

Diagnose Situation and *Manage Self* may be the most difficult of the four civic leadership competencies to grasp because they require us to question deeply held convictions about what's happening and what we should do. They also require us to scrutinize our own personal strengths and weaknesses and leadership capacities. Initial impressions and intuitions about a situation are often misguided and, frankly, biased. Because they are our own, it is much harder to overcome them. It takes looking through a different lens to see the distinctions between technical and adaptive work and to discern the differing, usually conflicting, points of view of the various factions. Making observations and testing different interpretations help us make conscious choices about what actions will make progress on the issues we care about.

As we've seen with each of our exemplars, the ability to discern what's really going on comes easier to some than to others. Lance Carrithers had an uncanny knack for opening himself to the deeper and darker interpretations of what was happening in Dodge City. Perhaps what allowed him first to acknowledge and then to contemplate the more troubling aspects of the situation evolved from the coupling of an outgoing and inquisitive personality and his spiritual practice. A consummate politician, Doug Mays instinctively recognized the internecine tensions and struggles of partisan politics. Understanding these dynamics then helped him counter his own tendencies to react angrily to challenges and provided time for alternative approaches to emerge. By taking the time to step back to diagnose what was going on in Allen County, David Toland was able to make the critical, perhaps counterintuitive for him, distinction between content and process challenges. Doing so allowed him to move away from technical approaches to improving health to find ways of engaging many more of his fellow citizens to take responsibility for their own and their county's health. And, sometimes, as Laura McConwell learned, an unexpected challenge like her confrontation with some of Mission's residents over the "driveway tax" reinforces the importance of taking the time early on to discover the "below the surface" tensions that characterize most civic situations.

We have also learned through our experience that the discipline of diagnosing a situation can be developed. Cultivating this capacity is especially necessary for those of us involved in civic leadership. There is no question that civic challenges are always embedded in a larger, complex, multifaceted social and political context. Effective leadership, then, requires a deeper understanding of this larger context and of its implications for engaging others, as well as getting a grasp of the immediate situation. As has been noted, the civic arena with its multiple factions and diffuse authority, poses far more barriers to exercising leadership than the more hierarchical organizational settings we often encounter. A deeper diagnosis provides the insight we need to intervene skillfully and successfully in these challenging situations.

Diagnose Situation

Exercising civic leadership requires a deep understanding — a diagnosis — of the context and challenges of a particular situation. This is an ongoing process of reexamination and questioning your own and others' closely held assumptions about and interpretations of what's going on. Gathering data, making observations and testing various interpretations of what's happening helps you make conscious choices about how and when to intervene.

- **Explore tough interpretations**
  - Most of us tend to gravitate to benign interpretations of what's happening. More difficult interpretations may be too conflictual for us to want to consider. What about you either helps or hinders your considering tougher and more challenging interpretations of what's going on?
  - In a given situation, what stories about how events might unfold make you really uncomfortable?

- **Distinguish technical and adaptive work**
  - Adaptive challenges are pervasive in the civic arena. It's easy to misdiagnose an adaptive challenge as a technical issue. After all, technical challenges seem to be clearer, and thus easier to address. How would you distinguish a technical problem from an adaptive one? How would you counteract the tendency to identify and characterize civic concerns as technical rather than adaptive challenges?
  - In a given situation, what are the technical and what are the adaptive challenges?

- **Understand the process challenges**
  - Process challenges relate to how people work together to address a problem, issue, or concern rather than the content. What makes it challenging for you to work with others?
  - In a given situation, what helps or hinders how different factions work together? What makes leadership difficult?

- **Test multiple interpretations and points of view**
  - Multiple interpretations of what's going on abound in any context, especially in the civic arena. How might you identify and then test the accuracy, plausibility or popularity of the different ones you encounter?
  - In a particular situation, what are the stories about what's happening that are at play? Who can help you test the accuracy and plausibility of these stories?

- **Take the temperature**
  - In any situation requiring leadership, it takes pressure and heat to make progress. Too little heat leads to no progress. Too much heat can blow the situation apart. How might you assess the level of pressure or heat in a given situation?
  - In a given situation, what's the level of energy, pressure and heat around the concern? Will you have to raise the heat or lower the heat to help move ahead?

- **Identify who needs to do the work**
  - When working with adaptive challenges, many people are part of the problem and share some responsibility for making progress. Our tendency is to focus on the dominant or more prominent factions — the usual voices — leaving out others with lesser roles, influence or status. What ways can you imagine that would help you consider a broader range of stakeholders?
  - In a given situation, whose problem is it? Name the factions that are involved. Describe the values, interests and aspirations of each of these factions. How do these values, interests and aspirations compare, complement or conflict with each other?

Chapter 6
Intervene Skillfully

The true measure of leadership must be that actions — or as we characterize them more specifically, *interventions* — change circumstances over time and lead to progress. These change-inducing actions begin with someone who cares enough to become personally involved in an issue and, along the way, is willing to work with the inherent risks of leadership that inevitably crop up.

We define a leadership *intervention* as an orchestrated attempt by one or many people acting to influence what happens in order to make progress on a shared concern. To *Intervene Skillfully* is to do so in a conscious, intentional and purposeful way. We become conscious and intentional by assessing, then diagnosing the situation and conducting ourselves in appropriate ways, thus managing self. Progress is made, then, by intervening in ways that engage and energize others around a collective purpose. Some might characterize this as being the point at which the rubber meets the road; we would agree.

Adaptive work, and therefore civic leadership, requires engaging others and working across multiple factions where no one perspective or ideology is sufficient for true, lasting progress to be made. It's essential to recognize that in these situations conflict is part and parcel of the process, although sometimes too much of it inhibits the capacity to work together, while too little keeps the pressure to change or adapt too low. It's also good to note here that there are times when conflict, when so buried in a situation that it's hidden, gets in the way of progress. But skillful interventions help manage conflict, at whatever level it exists, by bringing it into the open and working through it in a productive way. There's no question that this is risky business both personally and professionally. Making conscious choices about how to intervene makes us assess and accept how much risk we're willing to take to act in the service of what we care about.

Making progress on adaptive challenges in the civic arena takes innovation and experimentation. It is necessarily incremental, coming from the cumulative impact of many smaller interventions over time. Aspirations for large-scale change begin small, with experiments that start a movement toward longer-term adaptations. And as realistic advocates for change, we must keep in mind that there's no way of knowing whether an intervention will work until we try it. If it works, great, then we move on to the next one. If it doesn't, we evaluate why, adjust the approach and try again.

Civic leadership is at once a discipline and an experimental and improvisational art, as we'll see in considering an evening in Mission Mayor Laura McConwell's fourth term. If one cannot become comfortable with leadership's inherent uncertainty and ambiguity, success is not likely to follow.

Many of the people in the hostile crowd confronting Mayor McConwell had come to protest the city council's recent decision to charge what amounted to a user fee to help fund new road repairs and maintenance. They viewed this decision as a bolt out of the blue, an unexpected and isolated action that could further stagnate and crush economic growth in the community. The mayor had come to the historic Mission Theatre that evening thinking she was there to explain why the Transportation Utility Fee was necessary, how it fit with the city's longer-term goals, and how it would work. But rather than giving her well laid-out presentation for a fee that she assumed had widespread community support, she found herself instead in the midst of a firestorm of angry constituents, fists shaking, one shouting out over another. She tried hard to keep her cool and manage the conflict flaring up from those sitting in the seats and standing in the aisles of the old theater. It was, to put it mildly, not one of the more enjoyable evenings of her time as mayor.

For McConwell, the decision to implement the fee had certainly not been hers alone, nor was it the only council-approved funding source; rather, it was one of a package of several options for paying for the badly needed improvements to the city's roads and bridges. The improvement measure was the logical outcome of a visioning process, completed in McConwell's second mayoral term, which had identified areas of community concern and established priorities for tackling them. The agreement coming out of that process had set the context for future action in several areas.

But, despite the groundwork laid by McConwell in that visioning effort and the actions that followed it, when the full financial implications of the priorities began to emerge, controversy arose right along with them. As the primary buffer between Mission's city council and the public, the mayor found herself repeatedly under fire from different groups, including many who had had a say in the earlier visioning process. The analytic bent of McConwell's lawyerly mind was surprised and somewhat mystified by the seeming breakdown of the logical steps she and city council had taken to ensure that the public had been included in the process all along the way.

That second-term community visioning process was, in fact, the first significant intervention of McConwell's mayoral career. She'd come to office following the death of her influential and well-liked predecessor, an individual some believed had been less willing to raise more controversial concerns. The benign neglect of the city's decaying physical infrastructure was one of the challenges McConwell had identified as of major importance upon taking office. From her perspective, Mission was an aging community at a crossroads, one that had some problems, of course, but was showing signs of redevelopment. She wanted to capitalize on those up-trend signs and reasoned that if the citizens wanted to attract people to come and invest their hard-earned money, the city needed to have the infrastructure to support that. The visioning process offered her an opportunity to escape the shadow of her predecessor and establish herself as a credible actor in and for the city. Her considered decision to begin in that way would, she hoped, give her a rationale and platform for future actions. Her intent was to be a proactive mayor in setting a course for her city and pragmatic in follow-up by experimenting with and adjusting her approach as needed.

As part of her proactive approach and to follow up on the earlier visioning process and listening sessions, McConwell and the city administrator put together several community forums, some attracting up to 70 people, and drafted a survey to check that residents really did, in fact, want the city to fix the streets. The general consensus, as they read it after those meetings, was that most citizens viewed the improvements as essential to achieving the earlier vision for Mission's redevelopment.

The more volatile question, she'd known from the get-go, was going to be how to pay for it all. The way she saw it, the Transportation Utility Fee proposal would be an early test in her latest term of the depth of agreement about priorities and her capacity to hold to purpose.

Early on in that fourth term, McConwell was put on the defensive by a flurry of hostile emails, many from outside the city, after the fee option was first announced. Not entirely surprised by this, she tried to explain the measure and reassure citizens that they'd be kept informed every step of the way. But she was surprised, and dismayed, by how quickly misconceptions took hold in the community and how heated reactions became.

On local talk radio the purpose of the fee — which soon came to be called by nearly everyone in town "the driveway tax" — and how it would be assessed were called into question. Day after day, one irate caller after another voiced his or her scathing opinion of both the fee and the mayor. To McConwell, the whole thing seemed to take on a life of its own, particularly when the issue began to garner national attention in the anti-tax community. She began to think that somehow she'd landed on some planet other than her own.

To try to stay ahead of the growing controversy, the mayor and her city administrator convened two more community forums. With these interventions, they wanted to clarify the proposal for the fee and explain how it fit with the city's aspirations and other funding options, as well as give citizens every opportunity to consider and discuss all of what was being proposed. Each of these gatherings attracted about 50 people, though it wasn't clear how accurately they represented the different factions in the community. At each forum city staff helped inform and facilitate small group discussions using different-size wedges in a "pie exercise" to help participants visualize the different options for raising the needed $1.5 million: increase sales taxes, raise property taxes, assess the Transportation Utility Fee, make special assessments on property owners directly along the affected streets or cut city services. They pointed out how each of the options would affect citizens in different ways, with the financial burden falling more heavily on some than on others no matter where the monies came from. Understanding the potential effects — losses — and speaking to those affected, the mayor and city administrator believed, would be crucial in gaining the civic will to support whatever decision the council wound up making. Given the varying impacts and well acquainted with Mission's residents, the administration also knew some people would oppose whatever that decision was.

When the forum exercises ended, most of the groups concluded that the fee, the TUF, should be used as one of the revenue sources, but estimates of how much of the total funding need it should cover varied from 10% to 50%. Averaging those estimates, the city's staff and council decided that the Transportation Utility Fee option should be included, with about half of the total needed revenue coming from it. Accordingly, by a vote of 7 to 1, the council later approved its inclusion. McConwell had been relieved; everyone seemed pleased and prepared to move forward.

But within days of the approval vote, her relief turned to low-grade alarm when the mayor found herself under those dim, shadowy lights of the old Mission Theatre, trying to beat back the flames ignited by a crowd of citizens mostly hostile to the implementation of the "driveway tax." In planning the community meeting, she'd thought having it away from council chambers in a neutral setting might defuse some of the tension that had begun to build again or at least create a more conducive environment for sharing information and correcting misperceptions. Going in, her plan was to deliver her presentation, meant to clarify exactly what the TUF was and what it would mean for Mission's citizens, as well as outline the options any citizen had for appealing council's decision. But the best-laid plans oft go awry, she told herself with a pang, as she soon saw how wrong she'd been to assume how things would go; obviously, the vast majority of attendees had come to rant and rail against the decision, not support it, no matter what. Despite the forums held over the past few months, a number of participants claimed they hadn't heard word one about the process, while some felt the fee should be put to a public vote.

In fact, a few had come looking for a better understanding of what the fee was all about, but the rancor of those who were opposed completely overshadowed them. At some point, while standing on that stage dodging fireballs, as she wished she were at home eating a bowl of ice cream, or anywhere else for that matter, McConwell tried her best to be the voice of calm. Standing before the agitated crowd, her goal was to resist the uproar while holding to the community consensus for redevelopment, the one that had emerged through the stages of the earlier public engagements. Though a lot of invective was hurled her way that night, she counted herself lucky that none of it landed along with a rotten tomato.

A year later, much of the street work envisioned earlier was in process or completed. The re-greening of the city had begun and a ¼-cent sales tax had been approved in a ballot measure in 2011 to complete the financing. The heat of the flames thrown that night at the Mission Theatre had dissipated, but the controversy over the "driveway tax" hadn't completely died away. A vocal minority still berated the mayor for spending too much money during economic hard times, but the noticeable and generally well-regarded improvements seemed to have taken much of the sting out of the opposition.

The mayor's first significant intervention, the visioning process in her second term, had set the stage for future interventions and real progress — the community forums, the vote on the funding options, even the Mission Theatre meeting, then the commencement of work on the streets. Each one responded to the conditions emerging from the previous intervention. Each one represented an experiment with unpredictable outcomes; each, in KLC terms, turned up the heat — sometimes a little more than was expected — and each gave some of the work back to citizens. At every step, the mayor, the city administrator and the city council held to the stated purpose, spoke from the heart about what they were seeking and made reasoned, conscious choices about how to proceed. But without the consistent focus provided by that early, broader consensus supporting the infrastructure work, it's unlikely that either the mayor or the council could have continued to intervene so successfully and sustain the work.

In a profile written for the *Kansas City Star,* Laura Bauer referred to what people thought of McConwell's leadership, saying, "[She] has helped propel the city of Mission to a higher profile, even described by some as a progressive small town intent on remaining vital."[38] Mission's mayor believed in her city and was willing to intervene and take risks to ensure its health and vibrancy along with its sense of community.

An interesting parallel connects Laura McConwell's second-term visioning intervention with David Toland's listening tour that kicked off his work as executive director of Thrive Allen County. Though McConwell and Toland were natives of their respective communities, they both needed to establish credibility and enlist others in their efforts if they were to succeed. Neither of them knew to call what they did "leadership interventions," but that's what they were, and those initial actions helped them understand the motivations and loyalties of the various factions and the dynamics of the community around the presenting issues. From there, they determined strategies for future interventions.

Toland recognized that neither he nor anyone else there knew exactly how to get residents to take more responsibility for their own health and for the overall health of the county. If he and TAC were to make any progress, they would have to act experimentally, engaging others and feeling their way into viable strategies. Unlike McConwell in her position as mayor, Toland's role as executive director came with little authority and lacked the convening power of a mayor's office. If he were to engage others, it would have to be done one step — or intervention — at a time, with him meeting the citizens of the county where they were and slowly building relationships. The success of the coalition would be, for all practical purposes, what Toland himself could make of it.

Always the go-getter, he wasted no time getting started. Eager to reintegrate into his old/new community, a few days after his return to Kansas he attended a public meeting about a possible bond initiative to fund the replacement of the district's aging school buildings. Thinking that expanded school facilities would help support TAC's mission by providing facilities that could be used for health-related activities, he jumped headlong into the discussion by suggesting something big — that a new building should also benefit the larger community by serving as a community center. The next thing he knew, he was the chairman of a newly formed committee to study that possibility. His impulsiveness in this instance would come back to haunt him, though, when, in the wake of the near-collapse of the country's financial system, the energy to support the bond initiative deflated. Toland's ideas and enthusiastic support for the bond issue had suggested to more than a few Iola residents that the newcomer in their midst was a spendthrift and pinned on him that hard-to-shake label of the tax-and-spend liberal.

With no particular expertise in the health arena and few precedents for this kind of work, Toland had to be willing to experiment with new ideas and rely on his intuition to inform his actions. He figured if he were to try ten things and was right six out of those ten, then that would make six more positive outcomes than the zero there'd be if he didn't try. The way he saw it, it was like throwing a few spaghetti noodles against the wall; if the experiments didn't stick, they'd throw some more.

And some of those spaghetti noodles did stick. TAC and Toland knew they could make no progress if most of the county's residents didn't recognize the seriousness and depth of the health concerns. In KLC terms, Toland needed to raise the heat. In the spring of 2008, he contrived a loose four-way partnership among the city, the county, the school system and TAC to fund a survey of health activities and attitudes of county residents. The partnership helped spread the cost and diffused the risk stemming from those who felt the survey was a waste of time and money. The report that came out of the survey in the fall surprised many residents who hadn't recognized the seriousness of health problems in the county. The next spring, the Kansas Health Institute ranked Allen County 94th out of 105 counties in the state in terms of health determinants and outcomes. These surveys — *interventions* — helped TAC garner the attention it needed to continue the work.

Another experiment that stuck was Toland's effort to get his own board members to expand their vision for TAC beyond the county seat of Iola. He wanted the organization to be a visible presence throughout the county, countering the natural self-reliance of outlying communities. He eventually persuaded the board to hold meetings in other parts of the county, to change the bylaws to include voting members from outlying areas and, finally, to acknowledge the good work being done in other Allen County communities. One measure of the sticking success of those particular actions came one chilly November night at a TAC annual meeting and awards dinner. The evening attracted more than 240 people from across the county, far outnumbering any other public event in the area.

Perhaps one of the most positive and far-reaching, and certainly visible, outcomes engineered by TAC, Toland and the many people working with him was the approval of a ¼-cent sales tax increase for building a new regional hospital. In a place as poor and anti-tax-minded as Allen County, the project's election-year approval of 72% represented not only a successful intervention, but also the enormous power of collective action. The organization put all of its credibility on the line and went for broke, and it paid off in a big way for everyone. By progressing from small interventions such as the listening tour, surveys and holding meetings in outlying areas to larger interventions like the regional hospital, Toland and others began to build a "constituency for change" that could eventually improve the health of the struggling county.

Divining the intentions and motivations of others may seem like something of a black art for anyone in the Speaker's position. While constitutional and parliamentary rules constrain what a Speaker can do, when negotiating the delicate situation concerning how to proceed in the wake of Governor Sebelius' executive order, Doug Mays had to weigh many considerations before intervening. He wanted to know how the Democrats in the House, as well as his own caucus, would react so he could understand what it would take to gain their support. The Senate, too, would have to weigh in on the matter, and he wasn't sure what they were thinking. He didn't know if his actions as Speaker would compromise his credibility with the district he was elected to represent, and the public and the media could easily misinterpret or misconstrue his actions. He would need this diagnostic information to help him think through how to intervene.

Based on this information, he needed to figure out how he could create a critical mass of support to move legislation along or stop it if need be. He also needed to decide how to further his own purposes while guiding and facilitating the work of others. Weighing benefits and risks of possible actions was part of his role, as was the existential fact that he would never, ever be able to satisfy all or even most of the various factions and constituencies with whom he had to work. His capacity to exercise leadership in this role was on the line at every moment, and he needed to use all his wiles to ensure that such a fickle and sometimes recalcitrant body would act, and act as responsibly as possible.

Indeed, Mays guided the Kansas Health Policy Authority Act through the legislature with near-unanimous support, and soon after its passage Governor Sebelius approved the measure.

Lance Carrithers will tell you that an inherent, and vital, part of any pastor's role is helping others with problems of a spiritual or physical nature. If he or she is to find success in doing so, as in other walks of life when change is called for, action or intervention must follow. And when engaged in church matters and with congregants, it's especially important that the pastoral intervening be done skillfully, without patronizing or condescending. At all costs, Carrithers believes, the pastor must avoid any paternalistic inclination to take over work that should be done by churchgoers. Given the nature of adaptive work where the path forward is unclear, some interventions emerge from forethought, while others take advantage of opportunities as they arise. As he tried to convince, cajole or coax his congregation into more broadly accommodating Hispanics at First United Methodist, Pastor Carrithers found himself both implementing thought-out plans and making them up on the fly.

His planned, provocative sermons had put the cat among the pigeons when he asserted that the church's future could be in jeopardy if the congregation failed to reflect the diversity of the community; he knew what he'd said got the pigeons paying attention to that cat. In KLC terms, the heat had been raised, while predictably provoking resistance among some church members.

When he gave that first sermon, Carrithers had no active strategy in mind for moving the church to take specific measures to become more inclusive; rather, he simply wanted to keep awareness of Dodge City's changing demographics in front of his flock. But the playing out of an unexpected and innocuous series of events raised the stakes for everyone. The pastor of a small Spanish-speaking church came to Carrithers to ask if his congregation might hold worship services in a small, little-used First UMC chapel, explaining that they could no longer afford the rent where they were. Carrithers was more than happy to agree and welcomed the pastor and his small congregation. He thought little more about the situation until some months later, when the other pastor unexpectedly left. The Spanish-speaking group assumed its congregation would be forced to disband, but Carrithers stepped in to assure them that they were still welcome to use the chapel.

In the months the group continued to worship there, another option emerged, another of the opportunistic variety of interventions. The coordinator of Hispanic Ministries of the Kansas West Conference of the United Methodist Church, Sergio Tristan, suggested that if the tiny congregation were to join the church as Methodists they might get more support. Though none of the small group of worshippers knew much about the church, the idea of being part of a larger community was so attractive that they decided they wanted to join. A surprised Carrithers was delighted.

But bringing these new members comfortably into the fold, Carrithers knew, would take careful handling. He would have to distinguish the technical and adaptive elements of this challenge and orchestrate the interventions in ways that fit the situation. First came the easier, immediate technical fixes such as doing the children's story time in Spanish, setting up a soccer pitch on the church's lawn and hiring a Spanish-speaking coordinator for worship services. But the adaptive work necessary to create a truly multicultural congregation would follow in small, incremental steps — *interventions* — rather than through revolutionary change. Along the way, even though he knew the community and his congregants and tried his best to stay attuned to them, he found that sometimes he still pushed a little too hard, disrupting the process. At those times, he backed off.

With new Hispanic members coming into the church, Carrithers knew that in order to bring along the established church members, his interventions would have to become more provocative and intentional. Those actions, he knew, were also more likely to put his position and the long-term future of the church in jeopardy. He anticipated that some of the resistance would include subtle, surreptitious, perhaps even unconscious attempts to undermine the work, which proved true. When one longtime member asked him if he knew whether the new members were legal immigrants, Carrithers took the question for what it was: a way of diverting his attention from the deeper issues of social justice. He reacted quickly and transparently, saying that documentation was not his concern, but rather the core values of an inclusive, Christian community. He was committed to and willing to take the risks to act in accordance with his values. He was set on doing what was needed, rather than on what some of his constituents might have preferred.

Carrithers' approach was one of trying to make the contradictions transparent to create enough energy for change without blowing the top off the situation. Rather than trying to manage the responses coming from his congregation, he and his staff focused on their own reactions and the congruency of their actions with the values they espoused. After several years of trial and error, they became much more intentional about the way they intervened, developing benchmarks for progress and retaining a consultant and coach to help guide the process. As the good pastor's story exemplifies, doing adaptive work means learning and experimenting with interventions and finding one's way into strategies that work.

Without interventions, leadership means nothing. Intervening brings leadership to life by linking aspirations to the possibility of making real progress. To *Intervene Skillfully* builds on the disciplines of *Diagnose Situation* and *Manage Self.* It requires improvisation, experimentation, learning from experience and persistence. Successful interventions bring head and heart together, coupling good strategies with clarity and depth of purpose. Making conscious choices about whether, when and how to intervene most skillfully maximizes the possibility of making progress.

Mayor McConwell built a series of agreements leading from aspiration and direction to notable work on the ground. With each step, the going got tougher and riskier as the reality of ideas in action became clear. Without the clarity of purpose emerging from earlier agreements to guide her, the continual buffeting of opposing views could easily have sent her off track. With little authority, David Toland built a constituency for change with enough oomph to bend the negative trends in health indicators in Allen County. Over several years, his constant focus helped create the attention and raise the heat he needed to energize others to help with the work. His willingness to experiment and take risks turned TAC into a widely acknowledged force for change, contributing to real results. Given his role, one might think that Speaker Mays had plenty of authority to impose his will on the legislature, but in reality, parliamentary rules and the complex politics of a polarized state gave him little leeway. His interventions required careful calibration to maintain his fragile hold on an unwieldy body. And in Dodge City, changing demographics and Lance Carrithers' inclusive vision of Christianity compelled him to move his congregation to more engagement with the Hispanic community. Pushed by both his own values and some serendipitous circumstances, he and his staff built a multicultural church through creative improvisation.

Each of these stories entails both gain and loss. Progress wasn't made without some offsetting cost, and no one path suited everyone. Weighing the risks of intervening against a larger purpose and making conscious and intentional choices about how to proceed helped these four Kansans make progress on the concerns they cared about. The lesson in each case: progress is possible with skillful intervention.

Intervene Skillfully

The activity of leadership starts with a personal intervention. Nothing happens until someone takes the initiative. Making conscious choices about whether, when and how to intervene most skillfully will help you maximize your chances to make progress.

- **Make conscious choices**
  - Most of us react to situations in unconscious instinctual or habitual ways. Becoming aware of these defaults can help us make conscious choices to intervene in different, more effective ways. How do you commonly react (your default) to the leadership challenges you face?
  - In a given situation, what is the purpose of your intervention? What kind of intervention from you might help make some progress? How does this compare to or contrast with how you would usually act or react?

- **Raise the heat**
  - Leadership challenges, especially those in the civic arena, are inherently conflictual. Making the conflict visible can help raise the heat if managed in a constructive way. What is your default: do you tend to lower the heat, thereby avoiding conflict, raise the heat to an appropriate level where work gets done or raise the heat so much that it keeps people from engaging with each other?
  - Given your diagnosis of the level of heat in a particular situation, what could you do to raise the heat so some work gets done?

- **Give the work back**
  - What is your default: do you tend to go it alone (the hero, the Lone Ranger), rely on others to exercise leadership (defer to others) or mobilize others to help do the work?
  - In a given situation, what could you do to mobilize others to help do the work?

- **Hold to purpose**
  - Clarity of purpose helps orient and guide interventions. What helps or hinders your capacity to stay attuned to your purpose?
  - In a given situation, what might throw you off of your purpose? How could you reorient yourself to your purpose and get back on track?

- **Speak from the heart**
  - Speaking from the heart about what we care about helps energize others, communicating our care and concern. What helps you to speak from your heart or hinders you from doing so?
  - In a given situation, what is it that you really care about and how could you speak about this without affectation?

- **Act experimentally**
  - There's no certainty about how to make progress on adaptive challenges. This means that one must anticipate the unexpected and be prepared to improvise and experiment. What keeps you from being more experimental in the way you exercise leadership?
  - In a given situation, what experimental interventions might you undertake in order to make progress?

Chapter 7
Energize Others

In a fall Friday evening scene that plays in most any town in any part of America, we see the hometown high school football team come charging onto the field, fired up and ready. Along the sidelines the cheerleading squad kicks, chants and yells its loudest to urge the players on and rally supporting spirit from the crowd in the stands. We all know it's possible for that spirit, the shared energy of the crowd, to make a difference in the game, occasionally *the* difference.

But when it comes to working on adaptive challenges in the civic arena, there's a great deal more to energizing others than the generating of crowd energy. Doing that work involves going beyond cheering from the sidelines or persuading others to do what we think best and want them to do. Success in this tricky realm comes when *all* involved take real responsibility for doing much of the work, when all of the factions are genuinely and appropriately engaged. Progress requires authentic engagement to help shape what needs to be done and then to act. That engagement must come from both the usual and unusual voices — those who customarily bring influence and expertise as well as those most directly affected yet usually overlooked. Bringing together the full range of relevant experience and knowledge makes progress more likely.

It's critical to recognize that time, experience and insight are required in any circumstance where leadership is required, especially when many individuals are involved and no one has the power or authority to act unilaterally. It all begins by acknowledging the current situation and how people view it as well as recognizing and speaking to the possible gains and the painful losses that change may produce for those involved. This is not content but rather process work, the central challenge of which is to connect and reconcile disparate interests in constructive ways that lead to progress. To be conscious of these dimensions and to intentionally work with them is a discipline that can be learned, but it's one that requires full measures of persistence and experimentation.

Cheering from the sidelines is certainly welcome and appreciated, and can be helpful in some ways, but progress is made only when the players are all out on the field, have shared in crafting the game plan and are fully engaged in playing the game itself.

Accepting the position as executive director of Thrive Allen County, David Toland knew his role would not be one of cheering from the sidelines; in fact, he expected to be on the field most of the time. And he knew he'd need the help of a full complement of players out there with him. Endemic poverty, a 100-year history of slowly declining population and the 94th-worst health ranking out of the 105 counties in the state were just a few of the adaptive challenges he faced. As one wag put it to him, it would be hard to find another place that was "older, sicker and poorer." His mission was to overcome these long years of stagnation and decline. Yes, he knew he'd need lots of help.

What complicated his task was that the health issues implicated every person in the county and that any significant improvement would come primarily from changes in behaviors. He also appreciated that developing complementary policies, programs and infrastructure could help support these behavioral changes. The reality was that unless the county's citizens learned to eat better, exercise more and take better care of themselves in general, no amount of treatment or health services were ever going to mitigate the debilitating effects of bad habits and unhealthy behavior patterns. Without individual personal acceptance of this fundamental philosophy and a widely shared sense of purpose for improving the health of all, the initiative was unlikely to succeed.

Clearly no place for top-down, directive leadership, Toland knew no one would be willing simply to follow his, or the organization's, instructions to become healthier, let alone accept a set of guidelines telling them what they needed to do to accomplish that. He understood from the start that he and TAC would have to find people who would use their influence and expertise to help build coalitions that would energize the citizens themselves to do this work. In this, he saw his role as being the one to give the coalition members a push.

Ever the one with a vivid imagination, Toland pictured himself standing behind a line of little go-carts waiting to be fueled up and for drivers ready to drive them. Tanks full, he'd find people to get behind the wheels of those carts, each one representing a different project, then give them a good hard push to get started. And off they'd go. The way he envisioned it working from there, the drivers would let him know when they needed a fill-up or maybe another push. Aware that he'd need to be realistic, he figured there was a chance some of the carts would stop mid-track because they just didn't have the right driver, or somehow would have headed in the wrong direction or maybe because he hadn't pushed them hard enough to begin with. He knew how his approach could look, certainly how he wanted it to look, but he knew there were no guarantees it would work out this way. So, to keep from becoming demoralized if some of those carts didn't go anywhere, he told himself he'd try to focus on the ones that kept moving, kept going forward. And he would try to remember to remind himself that before TAC, what carts there'd been had been few in number and not moving very fast at all.

Before his arrival, TAC had focused on providing a number of services directly to individuals — transportation to health care providers, dental and eye screenings and the like — services that were both welcomed by citizens and helpful to them. We would categorize these as technical solutions to technical problems, the marshaling of resources and expertise to treat obvious needs directly. Toland, who had no background in health care, epidemiology or health statistics but was fired up by his larger, more encompassing vision of a healthier Allen County, did not focus on the programs already in place. Instead, he started out pushing an agenda of wellness and public education, a decidedly adaptive approach. And push he did; he wanted to get people in those carts and was revved up and ready to get them going. But in doing so, what he found was that his impatience — his old can-do, get-it-going-and-done attitude — led to surprising resistance from some of his own board members. They'd had their own vision of what TAC's work should look like going forward, and at times it conflicted with Toland's.

After one particularly acrimonious encounter, he pulled up, drew a breath — or two or three — and took a step back to assess. He saw that what was happening with the board was not about whether he and his vision were right or wrong; rather, he saw that his ideas were simply different from where they'd been headed before he got there. In addition, through an honest though somewhat painful self-assessment, it was also clear he hadn't been as respectful as he should have been. Those old defaults had again been in play, and he had to admit that, unfortunately, his earlier contrariness had cost him the loss of a couple of the founding board members. That had been a blow and a wake-up call for him, but luckily the remaining board members were willing to give him time and latitude to get on with the work. So, at that juncture, he doubled down on his self-management, overhauled the go-cart plan, and got back to work, committing to taking a much more inclusive path.

Once a general approach had been agreed on and set, Toland talked with more than 30 civic, educational and governmental groups across the county over the next year to let them know what TAC was up to and what they would be asked to do to help. Although he didn't know to put our term to what he was doing, these were his early steps in the energizing of others. Besides seeking support and disseminating information in those meetings, he also wanted to temper expectations about what TAC might accomplish; he was walking a fine line, he knew, between raising aspirations and promising too much. But he was willing to walk that line, raising people's aspirations and making them promises as he went, because he believed Allen County residents needed to feel a sense of urgency. That urgency would come only through education, which, he firmly believed, would lay the groundwork for the hard work yet to come. Almost textbook in his approach now, at every step he was engaging as many people as possible to make progress.

The various acts of Toland's own personal engagement took many forms, from mundane administrative duties to planning fundraising events and speaking at community meetings about the potentially tragic consequences of inattention to one's health. In this last, one of the most effective stories he sometimes shared was that of an uncle he revered. Phi Beta Kappa, brilliant, successful attorney and all-around amazing guy, his uncle just wouldn't get a colonoscopy. Toland told how his uncle's family members kept asking him to, but he always claimed he was too busy and, anyway, he was fine, felt just fine. Well, his uncle's death from colon cancer rocked the family, he'd say, again experiencing the loss every time he told the story. It had been crushing for his family, a tragedy. And completely preventable. He'd stop at that point, and in that pause he'd look around the room, making eye contact, making everyone uncomfortable, knowing exactly what he was doing. People had to understand, and then change their behavior, get colonoscopies, regular mammograms and wellness exams. People had to stop smoking. Exercise. But he knew these sorts of changes, cultural changes, really, took time to take root.

There was a long, long way to go before permanently instilling those patterns into people's minds and lives. An overweight man might be persuaded and then change his ways, doing better for 10 weeks, eating better and exercising more. But the next week he might fall off the wagon and be back in the buffet line for a second helping of chicken fried steak and a big dipper of that irresistible, cholesterol-raising gravy. A busy mother might be persuaded to pack healthier school lunches for her children, but what prevented the kids from trading away their apple slices and yogurt for a soft drink or candy bar? He and the others at TAC weren't sure how to make permanent the changes they knew had to be made; they knew only that it was a learning process for the people and the communities they were trying to help to better health, and that it would take time. This was adaptive trial-and-error work with no magic formula for accomplishing what they knew needed to happen.

Allen County, though, was not without assets that could help realize TAC's vision. The nonprofit sector and the schools had some good things going on, but with little collaboration or cooperation between these efforts, there wasn't much synergy. Once Toland had his plans up and running, the situation began to change; more was getting done because people were taking the time to sit down together to talk and listen, really discuss, what they wanted to do. In considering how to get to the next level, to bring about that widespread cultural change, Toland had understood that Allen County truly had to become a countywide coalition. And trust had sprouted everywhere as TAC became a presence in the county's communities, large and small. Toland and TAC had been successful all over the county in helping people feel that they were part of something special, and residents began showing some pride in their collective actions.

This delighted David Toland and made him proud of what he, the organization and the county's citizens were accomplishing. Still, he constantly cautioned himself to remain mindful of the enormous amount of work that remained to be done, recognizing that making progress on those sorts of challenges wasn't a matter of jumpstarting go-carts but required and depended on the energy and commitment of everyone involved. If he and TAC couldn't keep others constantly engaged, constantly energized, their initial good work could disappear in a flash.

No catalog of woes on the scale of Allen County's confronted Lance Carrithers, but recent trends hinted at future turmoil for him and his church. Yes, after moving to Dodge City and taking up his duties as pastor, it was apparent to him that the Spanish-speaking population was growing rapidly. And over time he'd come to grasp another, perhaps awkward, demographic truth: the white population was steadily declining. The better-educated professional and business people were choosing to leave the area, and if the trend continued, he knew, his church's membership, too, was bound to decline. This realization contributed another element to what had already begun within the church and to what became for him a church- and community-wide crusade: to integrate Dodge City immigrant groups into the larger communal sphere.

Some of the views and questions raised by the predominately white, long-term church members were not unexpected: "Are we going to start having to have more Spanish programming and speak Spanish?" "Are these people we want with us in worship?" "The community is changing, but why does our church have to change?" Because of such resistance, vocal and overt, energizing others in the congregation to address these questions would, he knew, take time, repetition and opportunistic circumstances for him to get their attention. And he would have to start where they were.

Acknowledging the initial lack of trust, Carrithers began by slowly building awareness among his congregants of the feelings and needs of the different factions. Over time, he hoped that the relationship between the two primary factions would grow from mere toleration to mutual respect and even affection. Once he'd created trust and understanding, then he could move faster and more concretely. One of the experiments he and his staff used to help boost this awareness was to recast as bilingual the worship service's children's time. Given the obvious innocence and joy of the children in this experience, it was hard for anyone present at those services not to feel a growing sense of empathy and camaraderie. Perhaps the children will lead them, was the pastor's thought, and build bridges across the gaps between families from different origins.

The Christian gospel, of course, provided Carrithers plenty of inspiration for working with this issue, and he wasn't above using it to motivate his congregation to act. He believed that every pastor worth his pay "learns how to call out things that are in need of change, to name those and call people to begin thinking about and looking at making changes." He'd long felt that the place from which he preached was his bully pulpit, and now he came to suspect that his congregants probably felt there was a bully standing in it. But he fervently wanted his to be a "prophetic" pulpit, one that called out for a different, better world. Speaking in that way, he could both identify the values behind his and his staff's actions and call out and speak to the losses his people were experiencing because of the changes.

But forward progress wasn't always steady; each step ahead was often followed by a step backward when resistance rose again. Sometimes it was just too difficult to manage, and Carrithers and his staff would have to back off completely and try something else. Despite the hard work they put into building a trustworthy process, some church members departed when the reality of the changes became apparent. If there was a strategy, Carrithers saw it as moving forward in small, incremental steps balanced with steady pressure to move people along. Every time, he and his staff made sure to weigh the risks, asking themselves if that step was worth it, if the outcome would be positive.

Well into this process, Pastor Carrithers recognized the social changes to which he still aspires could be a lifetime's work. One day he stopped short as he looked over a spreadsheet, having counted and tallied the number of his congregation at around 960 members. This number had remained constant for several years; though it now included a larger number of Hispanics, some of the longer-standing white members had either quit or moved. He also knew that, as significant as these numbers were, there were still a lot of folks in Dodge City (population 28,000) who hadn't connected with a grace-filled, loving congregation. Going forward, he wanted to be sure those residents felt they had an open invitation to come and be a part of this experiment to fulfill his abiding commitment to building an inclusive, compassionate community.

On this larger scale, if he and his staff can pinpoint some of the reasons for why and how their efforts worked, Carrithers believes this experience could benefit others outside of Dodge City. He wonders if they've just been lucky or if there's something worthwhile that could be replicated elsewhere. Moving a few people to embrace a multicultural, multiethnic approach to building a congregation in Dodge City could prove to be a catalytic story, Carrithers hopes, one that prompts — energizes — others to do this difficult work across the state. He and his staff didn't do what they've done only for the good of their church or, more crassly, saving their jobs; they also hoped they were playing some larger role in helping others in the community learn how to live together.

Of the myriad ways in which it's possible to *Energize Others,* many for Doug Mays clustered under the umbrella of supporting those with whom he worked. He'd always believed that success as House Speaker depended on his capacity to build consensus both within his own party and across political lines when possible. His belief was that engaging others brought more and better ideas to a situation, and in practice his approach was to identify what needed to be done, then solicit and truly listen to the opinions of others with the intent of bringing clarity to the situation. Collectively, through the confluence of ideas and people, he found, there was a much better chance of coming up with something that worked.

This was true not just for working with his own Republican caucus, but with the Democrats as well. Through years of experience, he understood that engaging those sitting on the other side of the aisle, even though they were in the minority, was critical for making progress on issues. The day he became Speaker, he invited Democratic Minority Leader Dennis McKinney into his office. Over a period of years they'd developed a good, honest and trusting relationship and worked well together. That day he asked McKinney to help him make their two jobs a partnership as much as possible. He explained that he wanted the legislature to work smoothly and pledged never to lie to the Democratic leader, that he would try to give him as much information as possible and would treat him and other Democrats with respect. McKinney responded in kind, saying that he couldn't ask for more than that, so he would gladly do the same for Mays. Mays then proceeded to build similar relationships with those in key roles in the Senate.

Having established good relations over more incidental issues made things that much better when it came to the bigger ones, like health policy. Carrying on regular discussions with the Democratic leadership was critical during the Kansas Health Policy Act (KHPA) negotiations, and Mays wanted to ensure that the Democrats were an integral part of the process all along the way; it was too important to risk those initiatives being seen as partisan politics.

The way Speaker Mays saw things, working across factions was simply part of the job. He had to work closely with his own Republican caucus, of course, and also with the House Democrats, the State Senate and the governor's office and executive branch — all while serving his own constituency back home. To do this well, he needed good personal relationships across the many dividing lines of his political life. He wanted to know who all the other legislators were, why they were serving, what motivated them and what their agendas were if they had them. He understood that his capacity to get something done would be built on his credibility with others and the extent to which they trusted him.

Finding something that both works as good policy and can be passed into law is incredibly difficult given the divisiveness of today's politics and the inertia created by the checks and balances of the political system. Time and again, Mays saw first-term legislators coming into the House with little or no realization of what it took to make law, vowing to change the government in the first month. Oftentimes after a few weeks, these same individuals would be climbing the walls in frustration. To become law, any legislative initiative had to pass through a lot of hoops in the system, along with suffering all the attendant dissension along the way. There were dozens of ways for a bill to die and only one way for it to pass: get the majority of votes of both the House and the Senate and the approval of the governor.

Nurturing this understanding of the system with new legislators ushered Mays into a mentoring role. On meeting first-timers, the Speaker would tell them that credibility was the currency of legislative work. If legislators had credibility, he'd say, they could get something done. If not, they would likely fail. He'd point out to them how, as new members, they'd come into the legislature with a certain amount of political capital but that it could easily be squandered by trying to impress people. Then he'd assure them that, on the other hand, they could grow their capital by learning how things got done and getting to know the people they'd have to work with. He'd end by telling them another thing he hoped they would remember, something he'd learned the hard way: There was always going be at least one person who knew more than they did on every single subject.

For Mays, whether it was new legislators or seasoned opposition leadership, energizing others centered on creating an atmosphere of trust and respect, qualities he hoped he encouraged through his reliability, transparency and small personal actions that set a tone of collegiality. A particularly disarming habit helped Mays connect with others, including those who might not want to like him: his insistence on calling others by their first names. At one point, there was a legislator to whom he couldn't seem to get close and who addressed him formally, always and only as Representative Mays. One day, the Speaker ran into this other man in the hallway, and as usual he greeted him as Representative Mays. Mays stopped, signaling the other to pause, and then outright asked him to just call him Doug, pointing out that was what his friends called him. After a moment or two of what felt to Mays like a pretty uncomfortable silence, the perplexed legislator finally said, "Uh, okay … Doug." And happily for both, personally and professionally, this small gesture marked the beginning of a better relationship.

Mays was able to bring similar changes in civility to the House floor. When he was first elected to the legislature, the place was "a madhouse." After his election as Speaker, he made a point of raising his concerns about how House members engaged with each other. He told them he thought they all, himself foremost among them, needed to be more considerate of others and to recognize and then remember that everyone was human. He hoped that each of them would at some time reach across the aisle to see if they could find something to work on together. At the time, this was a real eye-opener for some who knew Mays as an aggressive and partisan lawmaker; with a reputation like that, he knew he had to back up his request with his own actions. Toward this end, he and House Minority Leader McKinney made sure to be seen regularly up in front of the chamber talking to each other. They'd talk back and forth and joke around some so others could see that they were trying to get along. Eventually, some of these changes in relational attitudes took hold in both caucuses, leading to more positive energy and better engagement all around.

Just as Speaker Mays worked at improving how the legislature functioned, Mission Mayor Laura McConwell wanted to create a transparent process for the city that others could trust or, at the least, know that they would have their say and be provided with accurate information. She believed that working with others, including those with differing or opposing views, even if it meant conflict, was an inherent part of her role.

In what became a tense community-wide clash over funding for the city's infrastructure needs, McConwell began with the intent to maintain the initial momentum and agreement over the plan. Her thinking had been that, to energize residents, the city administration simply needed to get information out to them and then set up some public meetings to elicit their feedback. But later, after the information was out and the meetings held, when people began complaining about not being part of the process, she spoke to them directly and offered other ways they might engage, encouraging them to call her personally if necessary. She wanted Mission citizens to get beyond reacting and take some responsibility for moving forward. If they didn't like what the city was doing, she wanted them to speak up and engage along the way.

In her quest to make this happen, she took pains to help others understand both the gains and the losses this initiative might entail. When a business owner she worked with requested a meeting for himself and 10 others to talk about why they didn't like what was happening, McConwell's sense was that such a meeting would be a perfect occasion for the group to go after her. So instead of agreeing immediately to the meeting request, she went to the business owner's office to sit down with him, just the two of them, so she could present her thoughts. This impromptu one-on-one encounter went well and led to a more productive meeting shortly thereafter with just two people, the same businessman and another Mission resident and property owner. Both came away with a deeper understanding of where McConwell stood and acknowledged that the way she'd handled things was probably better for them than if they'd had the originally suggested, multi-person meeting.

After that, such smaller, more personal meetings became the standard in Mission. In not backing away from difficulty, McConwell was able to convert some of those who opposed her to the broader cause while keeping her core supporters firmly engaged. These actions helped engage others more deeply in the city's decision-making process and led to better and more sustainable outcomes.

Energize Others is one part of our system of four interlocking and reinforcing civic leadership competencies intended to help engage and mobilize others to make progress on adaptive challenges. Like the other three competencies, it is a discipline that helps us become more conscious and intentional in our practice of leadership by directly engaging others despite differences and resistance to change. Without this direct approach, differences magnify, limiting both progress and the healing that can emerge from engagement.

All the protagonists in this chapter came at energizing others in ways that helped them cope with and find success in their particular situations. Doug Mays had to create some level of trust both in him as an individual and across factional lines to move the KHPA initiative through the House and beyond. By connecting those diverse interests, he helped establish and build broader support. Laura McConwell went out of her way to acknowledge her opposition in Mission, providing opportunities for those opposing her to be heard and sometimes to be converted. These unalloyed gains wouldn't have occurred without her impetus to include, listen to and hear her constituency. Lance Carrithers was engaging usual and unusual voices — respectively, his traditional, predominately white congregation and Hispanics moving into Dodge City — in his efforts to build a congregation more attuned to the 21st century. He needed to inspire a collective purpose and create a trustworthy process while speaking to the losses the changes would entail. Accurately diagnosing the situation allowed David Toland to start where people were in Allen County, helping them understand the necessity of change and the possible consequences of failing to adapt. With this awareness, he could then help people gas up their carts and give them a shove to get things moving.

Each sought to connect others to a larger purpose that would impel engagement, the sharing of responsibility and, finally, forward-moving action. With conscious attention and skillful practice, engaging others helps make progress by dealing directly with resistance. Progress depends on it.

Energize Others

Exercising civic leadership requires mobilizing others to share the responsibility and work it takes to make progress. This means connecting interests across factions, attending to how people work together (the process), speaking to loss and inspiring a collective purpose.

- **Engage unusual voices**
  - Adaptive civic challenges, as well as those in other contexts, involve multiple factions. Engaging the "unusual" voices in these factions helps add new knowledge and perspective, induces apathetic voices to participate, dilutes the influence of the extremes and shares the work. What helps or hinders you from engaging unusual voices?
  - In a given situation, what can you do to identify and engage unusual voices?

- **Work across factions**
  - Making progress on adaptive challenges requires collaboration — working across factions. In what ways will you have to change how you exercise leadership to catalyze or facilitate collaboration?
  - In a given situation, how can you connect interests or build bridges between factions?

- **Start where they are**
  - We often assume other people's perspectives or experiences are similar to our own. What helps or hinders your capacity to understand the perspectives and experiences of others?
  - In a given situation, what can you do to build your understanding of the circumstances, perspectives, positions and desires of others?

- **Speak to loss**
  - Making progress on the concerns you care about means something has to change, and change involves both gain and loss. In most situations, losses appear greater than gains. Learning to speak to and acknowledge these losses helps others adapt to new circumstances. How have others helped you come to terms with the losses you've experienced?
  - In a particular situation, think about the losses other factions might experience because of your and others' interventions. How could you help others acknowledge and come to terms with these losses while at the same time communicating the need for change?

- **Inspire a collective purpose**
  - Shared purpose helps focus collective action. Shared purpose doesn't mean specific agreement about what should be done and how to do it. Rather, it may simply mean acknowledging the gap between aspirations and reality and the need to narrow the gap in order to make progress. The narrower we define an issue or problem, the harder it is for others to find the space to engage with us. To engage others means relinquishing

some control over the outcome. What are the barriers, for you, to letting go of control of specific outcomes to focus on a broader purpose?
- In a given situation, how can you frame the issue in an open-ended way to inspire and allow people from other factions to engage with you?

- **Create a trustworthy process**
  - The possibility of collaboration depends on the trust others have in you or in the processes you propose for making progress. Reflecting on your own experiences, what aspects characterize the processes you trusted? Those you didn't trust?
  - In a given situation, what can you do that would increase others' trust in you or in the processes you propose?

As a result of seeing the consequences of urban violence up close, Kansas City pediatric emergency medicine physician Denise Dowd turned her energies toward prevention. Her evolution in thought and action traces the Kansas Leadership Center core competencies: Diagnose the situation, manage self, energize others and intervene skillfully.

Dodge City United Methodist Pastor Lance Carrithers felt called to build a more diverse community of faith. In diagnosing the situation, he was determined to make necessary changes.

Aging municipal infrastructure is not a new problem for suburbs like Mission. But when Mayor Laura McConwell implemented a novel approach to funding needed improvements, she learned new ways of operating or intervening.

As Speaker of the Kansas House of Representatives, Doug Mays, Topeka, navigated the complicated public policy and political terrain of state-based health care reform. His story illustrates the challenges he faced in managing himself.

There may be no better example of an adaptive challenge than the nebulous idea of "community revitalization," as David Toland found out when he returned home to Allen County after a few years in Washington, D.C.

Leadership scholar James MacGregor Burns' ambitious vision expanded the vision of leadership beyond management, thus paving the way for the Kansas Leadership Center and others who aspire to his transformative vision. (*boston.com*)

Nearly a century ago, New England political scientist Mary Parker Follett foreshadowed contemporary thinking of today's civic challenges, distinguishing the influence of one person or group from the synergistic potential of joint action. (*odewire.com*)

John Gardner, who served six presidents and founded Common Cause, determined the existing civic culture too divisive for meaningful progress. He urged leaders of disparate or competing interests to act together on behalf of the shared concerns of the community or nation. (Carnegie Corporation of New York)

As longtime faculty at Harvard, psychiatrist/cellist Ron Heifetz (left) and politician/journalist/lawyer Marty Linsky (right) worked through the distinction between adaptive challenges and technical problems and described how each requires a different type of leadership. (Harvard Business Press)

The Kansas Health Foundation's mission to improve the health of Kansans necessariliy involves community-level work such as the 'Let's Move In Kansas Schools' program, which aims to increase youngsters' physical activity. After years of experience, the Foundation concluded that civic leadership — broadly defined — is critical to making progress. This thinking led to the creation of the Kansas Leadership Center. (Kansas Health Foundation)

The Kansas Leadership Center can trace its origins to some Kansas Methodists who founded what was then Wichita's Wesley Hospital in 1912. In the mid-1980s, the United Methodist Church sold the hospital, and the proceeds created the Kansas Health Foundation, a nonprofit philanthropy. (Wesley Medical Center)

The Kansas Leadership Center equips people with skills to make lasting, positive change for the common good. KLC is unique in the field of leadership development. Our goal is to assist and partner with Kansans to help them become more effective at exercising leadership, which will help make Kansas communities healthier, stronger and more prosperous.

Fourteenth-century Italian Renaissance painter Ambrogio Lorenzetti portrayed and celebrated the civic pride and communal responsibility citizens felt for their Tuscan city of Siena and its surroundings in *Effects of Good Government on the City Life*, a section of his larger *Allegory of Good Government*. Similarly, we can imagine the essence of a more constructive civic leadership that brings more attention to the common good. (*studyblue.com*)

Part III

The Heart of Civic Leadership

Chapter 8
Learning to Lead

The old myth that leaders are born and not made has slipped slowly into the shadows as, over the years, people from all walks of life have demonstrated the capacity to exercise leadership in a wide range of situations. We've shared the stories of a pastor, two elected officials and the head of a nonprofit organization in which they found ways beyond the limited authority of their formal positions and past experiences to influence the situations confronting them. The compelling thing about these exemplars was their willingness to figure out how to work through inherently ambiguous circumstances. None had a recipe or a set of step-by-step guidelines for coping with their respective adaptive challenges. One step at a time, all had to act their way into a strategy. To make progress on the issues they cared about, all of them often had to think on the fly and make conscious choices, take risks to see what worked and what didn't, then refine their approaches as they proceeded.

In considering how to exercise leadership more effectively, we've offered our four competencies as a guiding framework for evaluating the successes and misses of these civic activists. As we've seen in the unfolding of their stories, some individuals handled some of the competencies better than others. Laura McConwell's skill at intervening in the moment outpaced her ability to diagnose the situation. Lance Carrithers' provocative sermons helped raise the heat in his congregation while using the protection of the pulpit to counter his potentially paralyzing desire to be liked. David Toland's ability to diagnose the political dynamics of a situation sometimes exceeded his capacity to manage his tendency to act impulsively. And Doug Mays' tight self-control kept him focused, although it may have limited his view of other options for engaging the governor in developing alternative approaches to health care management. None were consummate masters of leadership — none of us are. Such people simply don't exist — yet each of them, with experience and conscious attention, became more purposeful, intentional and engaging in the way he or she exercised leadership. Each person had the courage to intervene in a challenging situation and made some notable progress that would not have been possible without skillful interventions. Their examples clearly illustrate that to make progress, leadership is an improvisational and experimental art carrying both personal and professional risks while offering no guarantees of success.

Those who exercise leadership are both born and made. Just as you can become more conscious, intentional and purposeful about exercising leadership, so, too, you can become more conscious, intentional and purposeful in developing personal leadership skills. This comes about through constant reexamination of both successes and failures coupled with experimentation, reflection, learning and integration followed by more experimentation, further reflection, more learning and so on. There is no ultimate arrival; it's a process, a repeating cycle.

As with any trek into unfamiliar territory, the journey of learning to lead begins with first steps. We may each have some innate leadership capacities but, as noted earlier, leadership development is intimately bound up with personal development; we all have the potential to continue to develop these capacities throughout our lives. Leadership can be learned through both personal experiences — that school of hard knocks most of us are already well acquainted with — and structured leadership development experiences. Such structured programs help increase awareness of the strengths and limitations of default behaviors and expand the range of potential responses to challenging leadership situations. When leadership is on the line, participation in this type of rigorous learning experience can promote and support development of the ability to reexamine and learn from one's own experiences.

With the intent to deepen your thinking about your own journey of leadership development, we'll introduce one final story into the mix. While the stories of each of the four civic activists you've read about thus far spotlighted various aspects of each of our four leadership competencies, the saga of Dr. Denise Dowd's years-long, convoluted struggle to learn how to lead offers a more detailed, step-by-step look at that ongoing cycle of experimentation, reflection, learning and integration.

Denise Dowd had a calling, a purpose in life, and she knew what it was.

As a pediatric emergency medicine physician, the need for injury prevention was seared into Dowd's soul one night early in her medical career. On what had been a relatively quiet shift so far, in the sudden flash of lights from multiple ambulances she and the others on duty in the ER that night had three critically injured children in their trauma bays, victims of a car crash with a drunk driver. Working under tremendous pressure, the team managed to resuscitate one child only to lose him to an unsurvivable head injury. The second child, a little girl who should have been in a booster seat, suffered serious abdominal injuries from an improperly fastened lap belt. The third, a toddler and also in critical condition, had been riding in an unanchored car seat. It's common knowledge that to best attend to their patients, physicians are trained to compartmentalize emotions, but even though Dowd knew she was doing everything in her medical power to save those three young ones, she felt herself close to being overwhelmed by the situation.

After having done all she could for the children, she saw their parents, also injured but not as seriously, and saw how distraught and traumatized they were. After that, finally with some time to think and cast back over what she knew of the accident, she began to recognize how many factors might have changed the scenario for that family. Not a single one of them had to do with what could have been done in a trauma bay. If only the two older children had been restrained with proper lap and shoulder belts and booster seats; if only the little one's car seat had been properly secured. Any number of ideas and feelings surged through her thoughts and emotions that horrific night, but the central, gut-wrenching lesson she came away with was that there *could have been* much different, better outcomes. If only. And it was the "if only" that stayed with her and grew into something more, something that gave voice to her calling and altered her life path.

Car crashes like that one, along with abuse, youth violence and other injuries, account for about a third of the visits to a typical emergency department. But over half of all trauma victims who go on to die do so before they ever get to the ER, meaning an emergency room physician never has a chance to participate in their care. For Dowd, as she continued her work attending to young victims in the ER over time, it became clear that the causes of their injuries were highly predictable and that an appropriate response to them had nothing to do with training trauma teams or building better hospitals. No, thanks to the evidence she saw time after heart-rending time, she came to understand that the only real, meaningful, long-term answer lay in *preventing* those injuries.

When describing Denise Dowd, some might say that she'd been destined for a career in medicine. Her training started early, as a child at home in Detroit in the 1960s. The eldest of 11 children — seven boys among them — in a "crazy, chaotic Irish-Catholic" family, Dowd refers to her childhood and adolescent years as being spent both taking care of minor injuries and trying to prevent other injuries, large and small. Family tragedies, too, shaped her: her mother died early and she later lost a sister to complications from drug addiction. She knew all too well the impact of trauma and violence.

Dowd's first formal medical training was in nursing; by age 21, she was a registered nurse. Not many years after that she went on to medical school, earned an M.D., and followed that with a residency in pediatrics and a fellowship in pediatric emergency medicine. Daily experience treating the young victims brought to the ER put her in a front-row seat from which she witnessed the impact of behavior and environment on people's lives. Increasingly, the immediate satisfactions of providing emergency care and sometimes saving lives simply were not enough. Fueled by a deep and abiding concern for social justice instilled in her by her mother and her Catholic education, Dowd became even more motivated to get to the heart of prevention; she wanted to make a difference, figure out some way to have a greater impact on the issue, and she felt that lay in the coupling of clinical work with a focus on the prevention of traumatic injuries. With that end in mind, she added a master's degree in public health to an already long list of impressive achievements and set about working to make her vision happen.

Two years after receiving this last degree and an additional fellowship in injury prevention, Dowd was hired by Children's

Mercy Hospital in Kansas City, Missouri. Her duties there were to be twofold, emergency medical work and helping the hospital embrace prevention. At the time, Kansas City was suffering near-epidemic levels of youth violence, with few, if any, reasons for it. Although unsure of the hospital's sphere of influence, she began to probe what the institution might be able to do to help address this issue. These initial inquiries helped Dowd begin to grasp the multifaceted, systemic aspects of prevention.

Her focus sharpened when a mentor showed her an article from the *Kansas City Star* that included a photo of every young person shot to death in the area over the course of the past year. Scanning the pictures, spread over three full newspaper pages, the mentor identified many victims as her former patients. This graphic accounting of the number of young people her colleague had treated astonished her. As she stood looking into those faces, so many of them smiling at the camera and unaware of how short their lives would be, Dowd reasoned that if she could track the medical records of those individuals, she might be able to identify some markers or patterns of development that could help her understand why those particular youngsters had become victims of gun violence.

Combing through hospital records — in the time before enhanced privacy laws — Dowd soon discerned a pattern. For many of the victims, the difficulties started early in their lives with abuse and behavioral problems, escalating to episodes of physical violence and chronic trauma as they grew older and ending in death at a young age. Supported by an understanding of epidemiology gained from her master's work in public health, she was able to put forth a powerful argument about the causes and effects of violent injuries in that population. Her thinking was that if she and others in the community could work together to figure out ways to intervene earlier in the lives of these young people, many of the violent incidents might be prevented.

Ever the good doctor, Dowd now knew she had a diagnosis for "her patient" and could begin to use her expertise to prescribe what should be done. The way to address the problem, she believed, was by employing a traditional public health approach to prevention: breaking down the issue into component parts to be studied, figuring out whom the problem affected, determining the risk factors and identifying which ones could be modified through the hospital's work, engaging partners in the community, carrying out an intervention, then evaluating its effect. She saw her role in this plan of making things better as that of a strong, persistent engineer who could set some metrics, lay out a coherent strategy and carry the torch. All she needed to do to achieve success was to convince others to do what she so clearly saw had to be done.

That was her read of the situation, but the reality of it, she found, was something quite different; there were multiple aspects she hadn't foreseen. Readers may already have identified Dowd's concern about injury prevention as an adaptive challenge and have begun to see that the approach she'd laid out was more of a technical response. She, however, at that time was unaware of the distinction and the many implications of it in practice.

From our vantage point, we observe the aspects she hadn't anticipated were process challenges that demanded at least as much attention to how to engage others as to the direct and indirect causes of youth violence. The internal dynamics of the hospital and the competing interests of different factions in the community simply did not allow for her technical, linear approach to work. She hadn't foreseen these kinds of complications to her vision and plans and, as it developed, had no idea how to proceed in dealing with those sorts of challenges. Her disposition and self-concept, common to many doctors — that she was an expert, the one suited to diagnosing and then prescribing a proper course of action — limited her capacity to distinguish, or perhaps even credit the existence of, the adaptive aspects from the technical elements of the challenge. Certainly at that point, in terms of leadership, she didn't have the learning, the concepts or the language to begin to tease out and address the different aspects of what the work would entail.

With the exception of her small team and the division chief who had recruited her, few in the hospital knew anything about violence prevention, while those who did understand and tacitly supported the idea in theory did not share the same sense of deeper purpose or urgency. Many other people and factions in the hospital held differing beliefs about the importance or effectiveness of preventive efforts. A significant underlying factor contributing to her difficulties, she found, was that because their hospital provided care for people unable to pay for medical services, any initiative that didn't generate revenue to help keep the doors open was easily subsumed or undermined by more immediate demands. Such was the case when the hospital opted to go in a different direction and fund the more medical-related initiatives of pediatric and renal care instead of renewing the grant that had started the prevention program.

Highly regulated, expert-driven, hierarchical and rule-bound institutions, hospitals don't mesh easily with the kinds of collaborative community partnerships Dowd and her team had imagined. It was far too easy, she learned the hard way, to get at cross-purposes with the hospital's need to work with its funders, elected officials and other influential stakeholders. In many ways, community-based injury prevention just was not seen as an appropriate topic for the hospital to fully endorse.

So, feeling she'd done what she could through the hospital and with little to show for it, she began to think that perhaps the timing just wasn't right.

Those years of struggle and frustration tested Dowd's capacity to accomplish the goals she set for herself. In trying her mightiest to marry the medical and the social aspects of traumatic injury, it's clear to us, though not to her at the time, that she was attempting to apply a one-dimensional, comprehensive approach to a multifaceted combination of technical and adaptive challenges.

Although her years of fighting the good fight and finding little success had brought her to the point of total frustration, Dowd still could not let go of her long-held aspirations to help prevent violent injuries. Consequently, she concluded that she needed to step back and revamp her approach, "completely retool" herself. With some distance, she began to distinguish her own purposes and interpretations of what was going on from those of others with differing motivations, incentives, perspectives and interests. This was a crucial step to becoming more strategic about how and when she might intervene in more skillful ways and a big first step in that overall retooling process. Taking a new position as director of research for her division at the hospital represented a shift of her attention to more of the internal work of the organization. At the same time, she began mentoring some of the new recruits in her division. She planned to confine her work on prevention to public speaking and serving on committees at the national level.

But when Children's Mercy Hospital appointed a new chief operating officer, a nurse with a deep understanding of the social determinants of health and an equally deep commitment to prevention, it was clear the high-level authority backing Dowd's earlier efforts was now present. The new

COO soon set up multi-stakeholder councils to address issues such as diversity and prevention, ones that couldn't be or weren't being addressed through the hospital's traditional organizational structure. Along with one of the hospital's nurses who was experience in violence prevention research, Dowd was appointed co-chair of the Council on Violence Prevention, an interdepartmental and interdisciplinary body established to guide the hospital's violence prevention efforts at the policy and programmatic levels. Her co-chair's relational skills, integrity, and consistently positive approach to her work brought vital energy to the council and greatly enhanced its credibility and influence. Dowd could not have been more pleased with these developments and the new direction in which she was headed toward addressing what was still so important to her.

Soon after its creation, the council co-chairs helped facilitate an assessment of the hospital's work and began by evaluating across factions. They engaged and brought together other stakeholders, people who held a piece of the problem — who were part of it — but rarely collaborated with each other. They engaged medical professionals as well as social workers, security personnel and patient advocates, including some who lived in the same neighborhoods where much of the violence occurred. In their effort to define the problems, they'd started without a predetermined agenda, something Dowd would never have done in years past; she realized at that point that she was now in uncharted territory.

Out of this work, they crafted an overview of what was happening in the community. In order to create a shared understanding of the situation, they asked others how they interpreted the problems within the hospital and what was being done about them. By doing that, they wanted to ensure that the hospital's actions would be grounded in and responsive to the real needs of the community. This collaborative assessment of the hospital's work led to the creation of four work groups under the council's aegis: child maltreatment, domestic violence, youth violence and a data group to help inform all the work.

Around this time, Dowd took part in a leadership development program at the Kansas Leadership Center. Using KLC's principles and competencies, she was able to look back and identify where she had misdiagnosed situations and poorly managed herself as well as point out where things might have gone differently. She also began to imagine how things might be done more effectively in the future. Sensing how she might intervene in ways that would energize others to share the work and the responsibility for progress was a conceptual breakthrough for her. The changes in her thinking and approach precipitated by that shift in understanding, profoundly resonant as it was in her life, would not be a one-time phenomenon, she was to discover, but an ongoing one.

She came away from her leadership program determined not to repeat earlier leadership mistakes; for one, the council was not going to get out ahead of the hospital's management with its proposed strategies and actions. She and her co-chair planned for a continuing conversation with upper-level leadership to check in and seek advice. They set up regular times to let others in the organization know what the council was doing and to seek guidance. She also now understood that whatever her personal positions were on prevention, people in the community saw her as a representative of the hospital. This meant she couldn't distance herself either from these perceptions or from the hospital's concerns about how she represented its positions on prevention. In addition, she had to become more politically attuned to working across factions in that highly structured, hierarchical organization, and saw the greater benefits in it. In some ways, for Dr. Dowd the council work was not unlike undertaking a residency in a new field. With her recent leadership program as the learning foundation, she felt that now she was getting the necessary on-the-job training to cement it. What a long way she'd come in the process of her "retooling."

As the council's work gained attention and momentum, Dowd and her co-chair were delighted and encouraged as more people in diverse roles in the hospital wanted to engage, enlarging the scope and depth of what was being done. The work groups were able to address attitudes that tended to impede progress — "But we've always done it this way," for instance — and develop a deeper understanding of the problems to create successful approaches to dealing with them. Versed as she was now in the concepts and language of KLC leadership, Dowd recognized the value of the "unusual voices" at the table, especially from those employees who lived in affected neighborhoods and offered perspectives outside of the experiences of the medical staff. She and her co-chair were astonished when, despite the council's lack of authority, others in the hospital began to bring a varied assortment of ideas about prevention to the council for approval.

Of course, because of the many different values and purposes at play within the hospital system, not all of their experiments were successful and not all of their proposals took hold. In Dowd's own division of emergency medicine, not everyone shared a common purpose of prevention. Some perceived working with other divisions as a threat to their autonomy and didn't respond well to the informal authority of the council. A comment often heard was, "Well, who are you to say anything?" The old, deeply ingrained conflation of authority and leadership meant that most people looked to the authority figure to tell them what to do and not, as the council was doing, ask them for opinions, help and engagement.

In trying to solve a problem and not being tied to any particular authority or agenda, over time the co-chairs found the council's lack of formal authority to be one of its strengths. Unlike in most meetings, when one could expect to hear the usual line or spin on an issue, their meetings offered an open space where group members were free to say what they thought. It was a way to think creatively about new approaches without worrying too much about the potential risks. Participants appreciated the opportunity to speak and to have their insights valued. And, hungry for this kind of engagement, they kept coming back.

Today, Dowd distinguishes what she has accomplished within the hospital from progress in the larger community and national arena. She readily acknowledges both successes and shortfalls. Within the hospital, she and the council have initiated processes and procedures that are making prevention efforts more focused and effective. They aspire to become a national model for family violence by building on the council's work and developing guidelines for what this means based on a study of children's hospitals throughout the country. The work groups continue to help educate others in the hospital setting about violence and what they can do to help prevent it. New residents in pediatrics are exposed to education on advocacy, prevention and the social determinants of health. Dowd believes these younger doctors are the key to the longer-term cultural changes that prevention requires.

Some big challenges remain. She and the hospital still struggle with how to effectively engage community members as well as other institutional partners, and the hospital must continually reconcile ever-tightening regulations about the quality of care with the imperative to take an active role in preventing violence. Resource constraints hamper the hospital's ability to influence health policy and to engage others in the community. Creating a larger vision and a shared purpose remain elusive in this large, complex and diverse organization.

As with all adaptive challenges — and violence prevention is a doozy of an example — there are all manner and number of interior, exterior, small, medium-sized and large associated challenges. As Dowd came to understand, there is not one easy, technical, comprehensive, quick-fix solution.

Dr. Dowd's toil in this area remains a work in progress. The same is true for her personal capacity to lead. Reflecting on her KLC experience and its impact, Dowd admits that coming face-to-face with her own shortcomings and finally understanding that many of the people she'd worked with saw her as more agitator than leader was central to her learning. This retrospective analysis also revealed a number of other important insights: that her default behaviors of drive and persistence, both positives in some aspects of her life, in that situation left little space for others to share ownership of the work; that she'd provoked those in authority positions when she'd challenged the hospital's priorities and strategies; that throughout the years of dealing with all the organizational challenges, she'd been "too hell-bent" on getting something done to pay attention to anyone else; and that she was simply too politically naive to recognize her personal limitations.

Dowd credits much of the success in her revamped approach to leadership to her revelatory experience at KLC, to the knowledge gained there and the tools she acquired through participating. She talks about having learned how to entertain alternative interpretations of why people behave in certain ways. Rather than ascribing their actions to some personal weakness or laziness — another of those persistent old defaults of hers — she probes deeper to understand differing motivations and interests. Whereas collaboration had been far outside her comfort zone, she learned how to increase her range of leadership responses by experimenting with new ways of intervening in a situation and energizing others.

Her story illustrates so well the fits and starts that characterize adaptive work, the intermittent, even ephemeral, nature of progress. Her approach to prevention is now much more organic than in the past, but her goal is the same as it has always been. She's more comfortable letting the work evolve, knowing that how she gets to the ends she seeks will likely be quite different from what she had in mind starting out. Instead of expecting results in short order and wholesale — revolutionary — change, she now knows that progress will be measured in small, evolutionary steps over a much longer period of time.

In terms of her personal development, she recognizes that she's become less confrontational and more intentional in the way she exercises leadership. She's more reflective and has learned to be patient before responding — not an easy task for someone as headstrong, goal-directed and impassioned as she is. To make progress, she's had to increase her range of responses, learn how to intervene in ways that engage and energize others, and to manage herself all the while. When she looks back, she sees her own self-righteousness as having been the biggest barrier to the retooling of her approach to leadership.

Learning to lead has been at the heart of Denise Dowd's journey. One powerful impulse sustained her through these transformations: she was unwaveringly clear about her purpose.

Chapter 9

For the Common Good

The exercise of civic leadership is often viewed as an individualistic endeavor designed to further one's own desires about what should be done to address concerns affecting us all. A much more appropriate view for the 21st century would be to reframe it as sharing responsibility for acting together in pursuit of the common good. One way of visualizing this would be to imagine an expanding circle of concern moving, for example, from self or self and family to the community and the region. This would involve both feeling and taking a broader sense of responsibility for civic concerns that recognizes our individual complicity in these problems, and thus our implicit responsibility for helping make progress on them. Feeling this responsibility, each of us would help initiate action with others on behalf of the larger community forming, in John W. Gardner's term, a constituency of the whole.

The Italian Renaissance painter Ambrogio Lorenzetti, in his captivating 14th-century fresco series *Allegory of Good Government* (see page 139), gives us an allegorical exploration of two themes common to the art and ideas of the time: justice and the subordination of private interests to the common good. In substantial detail, he portrays and celebrates the civic pride and communal responsibility citizens felt for their beautiful Tuscan city of Siena and its surroundings. The civic culture he depicts captures the citizens' mutual respect and their consistent concern for the common good over private interests, and his vivid images of prosperous people and a fertile countryside radiate the virtues he had observed: peace, fortitude, magnanimity, temperance, prudence, justice and felicity.

Similarly, we can imagine the essence of a more constructive civic leadership that brings more attention to the common good. Rather than a ruggedly individualistic pursuit of our own ends, many more of us would demonstrate a more expansive sense of care and responsibility for the communities and regions in which we live. Instead of limiting our conception of what civic responsibility means to that of a passive, law-abiding "good" citizen activated only when our own backyards are threatened, our first impulse would be to engage others to work across factions in the service of the broader good, reflecting the pervasive application of KLC's principles and competencies of civic leadership.

Going deeper into our vision, we would see many more people from all walks of life taking the initiative to exercise civic leadership in more purposeful, provocative and engaging ways. Toward this end, we've suggested that progress on adaptive civic challenges would be measurable and that we would see an increase in *bridging social capital* leading to a more inclusive and productive civic culture. The sense of reciprocity implicit in this kind of social capital would help make the inevitable losses of adaptive change palatable. We would have credible forums where people could come together to deliberate in constructive ways. New and more trusting relationships would help facilitate interaction across social and factional divides while building coherence and a sense of belonging. Learning together would lead to new understandings of civic challenges and previously inconceivable strategies for addressing them. These engagements would help create a critical mass of people with the collective credibility to hold implementing organizations and authorities accountable for acting on agreements.

These are descriptors of what we might see, but we often fail to recognize a more personally rewarding aspect: we become better people when we put these concepts and ideas into action. Perhaps this is why, for some, this work has such spiritual and religious resonance. We know, too, that these potential outcomes are not pipe dreams, the unrealistic expectations of recalcitrant human beings. We have the stories and experiences to know that civic leadership and civic culture can be profoundly different, reflecting the visions and ideas of the many key thinkers who have informed our work. We would realize, for instance, Mary Parker Follett's aspiration to help people develop their capacity to work together and their sense of responsibility for the broader community. Leadership would be transforming, as James MacGregor Burns described it, pursuing a higher collective purpose over the achievement of narrow, parochial ends. People catalyzing work across factions would lead to John W. Gardner's "networks of responsibility" in service of the broader good. Many more people exercising leadership would help shift the emphasis from position and authority to the activity of leading, freeing us from the fetters of more traditional, sometimes exclusive and narrow ways of defining leadership.

We've learned from our work in Kansas that exercising leadership in the civic sector poses more challenges than in any other arena — public, private or nonprofit — in the sense that there is so little capacity to use authority to compel others to act. While this observation grew out of our experience in a particular state, a closer look at the civic context in other communities, states or, indeed, the nation, would lead to a similar conclusion. A glance at any newspaper or news magazine quickly dispels the notion that these pervasive characteristics belong only to Kansas.

In our earlier discussion of the influence of four great social movements on the civic context, we highlighted in particular the dilution of power and influence of those in authority positions, whether public or private, and the increasing diversity of people who wanted and demanded a greater say in civic life. Over the decades, these changes have led to a more inclusive, yet at the same time increasingly polarized and desultory, civic culture. Today, perhaps because they perceive they have more to lose, those in more traditional civic leadership positions — the "usual" voices — still try to dominate the civic dialogue while the "unusual" voices either sit apathetically on the sideline or reactively protest the actions of the more dominant factions. These factions tend to organize around specific interests or causes, creating advocacy groups that pit one against another in a win-or-lose contest. The most vocal or strident of these may carry the day in "us" versus "them" battles, only to be outdone or undone in the next round, leaving behind more anger and frustration. This unending contest among parochial interests prevents finding common ground, leading to a vicious cycle of diminishing mutual trust and further undermining any sense of shared responsibility. Given the adaptive nature of most civic challenges, absent a fundamentally different type of civic leadership, this unhealthy and unproductive civic culture offers little hope for making progress toward the common good.

Over these early years of KLC's existence, we have continued to refine our understanding of this current reality along with our aspirations about what could and should be different. The Kansas Health Foundation believed, based on its experience with previous experiments, that more and better civic leadership across the state would lead to healthier communities. The foundation felt confident that a more conscious and intentional effort to develop civic leadership could close this gap, leading to the creation of the Kansas Leadership Center.

Our intent at KLC has been to create a state of tension between these aspirations and the current realities of civic life. Our purpose has been to resolve this tension in the direction of our aspirations, rather than letting the weight of the current situation keep Kansas mired in the status quo. We have asserted that to achieve these ends — to close this gap — we must cultivate a profoundly different kind of leadership. Our belief is that, pervasive and powerful, this different kind of leadership should be capable of making progress on civic challenges while transforming, through its practices, the default civic culture of the state. It should be more purposeful, capable of keeping a steady focus on the common good rather than on parochial interests. It should be more provocative, capable of raising the heat and moving people to do productive work on adaptive challenges. And it should be more engaging, capable of bringing people together across factional lines to collaboratively address the state's civic challenges. KLC's principles and four competencies of civic leadership provide the framework for realizing this vision of a different kind of civic leadership.

Thanks to our five exemplars and to the thousands of people we've worked with at KLC, we continue to learn what this kind of leadership looks like in practice and what it takes to make it effective, as well as which aspects of the four competencies people find hardest to put into practice.

At the end of each of the competency chapters, we introduced some contemplative questions we hope will help you along the path of learning how to lead in more effective ways. We tied these questions to specific aspects of each competency and designed them to help bring the concepts to life. Now we want to take a step back and offer some thoughts from our experiences at KLC about the principles of civic leadership that ground the competencies and how they might challenge you personally as you strive to make progress on the issues you care about. We offer these thoughts tentatively. They reflect our current, still evolving learning about what it means to exercise civic leadership well.

- *Leadership is an activity, not a position.* Someone has to start the action, and it might as well be you. Do *something.* Where you start is less important than that you start. Experiment. Move from low-risk to high-risk interventions, not vice versa. Once you intervene, you can never be sure of the outcome. If what you try as an intervention fails, back off, reflect and try something else. Keep at it.

- *Anyone can lead, anytime, anywhere.* Many of us find it easier to defer to or wait on others to act, yet each of us has the opportunity and the choice to exercise leadership at any time in any situation. You don't have to wait for permission from others or until you have the authority to act.

- *Progress starts with you and must include engaging others.* Making progress on adaptive challenges in the civic arena requires the involvement of others and working across factions, yet facilitating this work consistently ranks as one of the most difficult aspects of the four competencies to master. It may seem easier or more rewarding to go it alone, but a self-centered approach is doomed to fail. To facilitate means making working together — collaboration — easier.

- Part of diagnosing means building a shared understanding with others of the situation and the difficulties it presents.
- Part of managing yourself means understanding how others see your role or position in a situation as well as seeking feedback from others and changing course when necessary.
- Intervening will require you to raise uncomfortable issues with others, to experiment with different approaches to help the group make progress and to turn the work back to the others rather than shouldering the burden yourself.
- To energize others, you will have to engage diverse voices in problem-solving and decision-making while creating structures that help others work together and change course when necessary.

• *Your purpose must be clear.* Clarity of purpose provides a focus or way of orienting your actions. Seeking that clarity of purpose could extend to what you do with your own life or, more immediately, simply to the actions you take at a particular time. Even if you aren't clear about what you should do with your life, clarifying the purpose of your next intervention can help make it more likely to succeed; you'll be clear about why you're doing what you do.

- *It's risky.* Make no mistake: leadership is risky, both professionally and personally. It's also risky because leadership is necessary but not sufficient to make change. Making the choice to exercise leadership to try to improve a situation requires you to find a balance between the inherent risks and the potential benefits to yourself and others.

It will take a movement to transform our civic culture. We have always been aware that the best of efforts from KLC will not be enough to achieve this aspiration. Our work may be a beginning, a seedling that may grow, but by no means is it yet a fully grown tree. That's why KLC's strategies embrace the need to work with other programs. That's why we seek to expand the application of the KLC concepts and ideas through our many connections with those of you who have come through our programs, as well as why we've put all of our work into the public domain. We recognize that even these steps will not be enough to transform a debilitating default civic culture into something more engaging and productive. We need a movement.

When we think of a movement that could transform the civic culture, we think of the American experience in the great social movements that led to such profound changes in this country's civic life. Constructed from the bottom up, these movements built from small successes to larger impacts over time. They connected and linked thousands of people with similar concerns. They informed and educated whether people were supportive, in opposition, or even disengaged. Their actions — *interventions* — focused on a few themes but took many forms stirred by the imagination of participants.

We can imagine a movement that embodies such qualities yet might differ in subtle but distinct ways. These historical movements were often unified by a powerful combination of charismatic leaders, a compelling sense of purpose and a deep commitment to a particular cause. The movement we have in mind would, instead, rely on many people rather than a few to energize it. Rather than a particular issue, it would focus on the way in which we address these issues — any issue — in the civic domain, bringing people together instead of driving them apart, making progress instead of engendering stagnation. It would focus on a widespread recognition that something in our civic culture has gone amiss, gone awry, and that we can do better. It would focus on a way of exercising leadership that would open up the possibility of practical, pragmatic, and useful action by ordinary people in their own hometowns and regions. It would be driven by the recognition of our shared responsibility to a greater whole, a commitment to making progress through the application of more powerful ways of exercising leadership and a deeper connection with others who share these aspirations.

Right now this movement is nascent, still inchoate, the beginning of one more story. We've taken the first steps on a longer journey. Our challenge, for you and for us, is how can we, together, help this story unfold, this journey progress? How can we build a critical mass of people who share these aspirations, ideas, and leadership capacities? We've wanted our account of KLC and its philosophy and practices to be the start of a hopeful yet plausible story about how events could play out in American civic life. We've wanted the actions and strategies of KLC to illuminate how this story might progress in the civic arena. We've wanted the story to stimulate your imagination by providing new ideas for how we act together in the service of the broader good. And, we believe, through our experience, that this story is possible, knowing that many of you have already put these ideas into action, moving them from concept to practice and making progress on mutual aspirations.

We trust that the adaptive strategies and illustrative case studies we've provided here will empower you and your friends to join us. There's much to do and a long road ahead.

Acknowledgements

Creating this book, much like creating the Kansas Leadership Center, has been a collaborative effort. Although we put the ideas on paper, many colleagues, friends, partners and program participants informed and enriched our work.

We want to express our deep gratitude to the staff, faculty and board of the KLC who supported our work throughout the writing process. They gave us time and space to write, reviewed drafts and contributed to the development of the ideas. Participants in KLC programs contributed significantly to the book and enabled a revolving process — teach, reflect, modify and teach again — that strengthened the concepts in the book.

The Kansas Health Foundation's support of KLC in general and of this book specifically should be acknowledged. The foundation embodies many of the leadership concepts explored in this book, especially "give the work back," "act experimentally" and "choose among competing values." The steadfast support of the foundation board of directors and President and CEO Steve Coen inspire all of us at KLC to work for the common good. Previous foundation figures including Marni Vliet, Don Stewart and Mary Campuzano nurtured the idea of a center for civic leadership development for two decades prior to KLC's launch in 2007. Absent their commitment, the stories in this book wouldn't be told.

Five individuals share their stories freely in these pages, and for that we are extremely grateful. Doug Mays, Laura McConwell, Lance Carrithers, Denise Dowd and David Toland gave significant time and energy to this project. This book explores the good and not-so-good of their efforts. They understood they were to be held up as examples, not heroes. Their stories are rich with lessons for all of us to contemplate and make this book come alive. We are indebted to them.

Over a year into this project, Laura Goodman, our editor and writing coach, saved us. Laura guided us, her "gentlemen authors," with tender care one moment and ruthless honesty the next. She is what we needed and did her job well. Her heart is in this book, too.

Many others played important roles. Chris Green gave us much of the raw material with his case studies and interviews of the five exemplars. Mike Matson guided the effort from final manuscript to finished book. Clare McClaren designed the cover with the same creative flare she brings to all KLC efforts. Sarah Hancock's editing expertise helped refine the text. Many others suggested revisions that made the book better: Marty Linsky, Karen Humphreys, Doug Easterling, Richard Couto, Thomas Cronin, Stephen Fawcett and Stephen McCormick.

Carol Wilson and Joanna O'Malley patiently watched us struggle at the beginning of this process, hit our stride in the middle and surge to the finish. We are exceptionally thankful for their advice, love and encouragement.

Always in our minds are those early 20th-century Kansans who struggled to make their community stronger and healthier and by extension gave birth to KHF and KLC. Fittingly, theirs is one of the first stories of the book.

David Chrislip and Ed O'Malley
Wichita, Kansas
May 2013

About the Authors

In many ways, David Chrislip (right) and Ed O'Malley (left) are an unlikely pair to write a book together. David is a Democrat, Ed a Republican. Ed uses a PC, David works on a Mac. David is a cyclist, Ed a runner. Ed is in his 30s, David in his 60s. Because Kansas is Ed's home state and David has deep roots there, it's a place near and dear to both their hearts.

Although they share a deep passion for working for the common good, their experiences in civic life have been quite different. David's civic leadership has primarily been in multi-stakeholder, cross-sector collaboration at the community and regional level, while Ed's work has primarily been through government and politics.

David has spent 35 years engaging with the concept of civil society and in the work of civic leadership and collaboration. His career has taken him from the National Outdoor

Leadership School and Outward Bound to the American Leadership Forum to the National Civic League. He's worked with hundreds of communities and organizations across this country as well as internationally and has conducted leadership development programs for thousands of people seeking to exercise civic leadership more effectively. He is currently doing what he calls "culminating work" as senior fellow at KLC. He's also the co-author, with Carl Larson, of *Collaborative Leadership* and author of *The Collaborative Leadership Fieldbook.*

Younger than David but unable to keep up with him on a bicycle, Ed is a politician turned leadership developer. He's had a front-row seat to effective and ineffective civic leadership while serving as an aide to a former Kansas governor and as a young state legislator. As president and CEO of KLC, Ed is guiding an effort unlike anything seen before in America. In no other place has there been such a concentrated effort to cultivate civic leadership at an unprecedented statewide scale supported by such a high level of sustained funding.

A commitment to civic engagement and leadership development brought these two together at the Kansas Leadership Center. They've spent countless hours working together over the past several years, along with their many close colleagues and hundreds of Kansans engaged in civic life through the work and programs of KLC. This book reflects their experiences.

Endnotes

[1] Becker, Carl. "Kansas." In Ford, Guy Stanton, ed. *Essays in American History*. New York: Henry Holt & Company, 1910, p. 98.

[2] Ibid. p. 111.

[3] Ibid. p. 94.

[4] Drucker, Peter. *Management: Tasks, Responsibilities, Practices.* New York: Harper & Row, 1973, p. 17.

[5] Alinsky, Saul D. *Rules for Radicals: A Pragmatic Primer for Realistic Radicals.* New York: Vintage Books, 1971, p. 3.

[6] Hawken, Paul. *Blessed Unrest: How the Largest Movement in the World Came into Being and Why No One Saw It Coming.* New York: Viking, 2007.

[7] Carson, Rachel. *Silent Spring.* New York: Houghton Mifflin, 1962.

[8] Friedan, Betty. *The Feminine Mystique.* New York: Dell, 1963.

[9] Burns, James MacGregor. *Leadership.* New York: Harper & Row, 1978.

[10] Ibid. p. 20.

[11] Ibid. p. 20.

[12] Italie, Hillel. "Profile in Independence." *The Boston Globe*, Dec. 26, 2007.

[13] Burns. *Leadership.* p. 73.

[14] Ibid. p. 73.

[15] Follett, Mary Parker. *The New State: Group Organization the Solution of Popular Government.* University Park: Pennsylvania State University, 1998 (originally published in 1918).

[16] Metcalf, Henry C. and Urwick, L., eds. *Dynamic Administration: The Collected Papers of Mary Parker Follett.* New York: Harper, 1942, p. 99.

[17] Follett. *The New State.* p. 19.

[18] Ibid. p. 367.

[19] Gardner, John W. *Leadership: A Sampler of the Wisdom of John Gardner.* Minneapolis: University of Minnesota, 1981, p. 29.

[20] Ibid. p. 19.

[21] Peirce, Neal and Johnson, Curtis. *Boundary Crossers: Community Leadership for a Global Age.* College Park, MD: University of Maryland, 1997, p. 10.

[22] Ibid. p. 22.

[23] Ibid. p. 34.

[24] Ibid. p. 28.

[25] Bennis, Warren. "The Challenges of Leadership in the Modern World."

American Psychologist. Volume 62, Number 1, January 2007, pp. 2–5.
[26] Burns. *Leadership.* p. 19.
[27] Kleiner, Art. *The Age of Heretics: Heroes, Outlaws, and the Forerunners of Corporate Change.* New York: Currency Doubleday, 1996, p. 30.
[28] Ibid. p. 38.
[29] Ibid. pp. 34–35.
[30] Kotter, John P. *A Force for Change: How Leadership Differs from Management.* New York: Free Press, 1990, p. 3.
[31] Ibid. p. 3.
[32] Ibid. p. 4.
[33] Ibid. p. 5.
[34] Heifetz, Ronald A. and Sinder, Riley M. "Political Leadership: Managing the Public's Problem Solving." In Reich, Robert, ed. *The Power of Public Ideas.* Cambridge, MA: Ballinger, 1988, p. 194.
[35] Heifetz, Ronald A. "Adaptive Work." In Bentley, Tom and Wilsdon, James, eds. *The Adaptive State.* Demos: London, 2003, pp. 70–75.
[36] Roosevelt, Theodore. "Citizenship in a Republic." Speech. Paris, France, April 23, 1910.
[37] *Kansas County Health Rankings 2009.* Topeka, KS: Kansas Health Institute, 2009.
[38] Bauer, Laura. "Mayor Laura McConwell has a Vision for the City of Mission." *The Kansas City Star,* February 16, 2012.

Index

D

E

F

G

H

M

N

O

P

R

S

T

U

V

W

Y

CPSIA information can be obtained
at www.ICGtesting.com
Printed in the USA
LVIC07n0410240813
349450LV00001B
9780988977709